The Little Book of Belfast

Raymond O'Regan
& Arthur Magee

For Adrian, Elizabeth and
Rudy & Martha,
Martha Rose and Stephen

In memory of Dr Eamon Phoenix,
historian and friend

First published 2014, second edition published 2015, this paperback edition published 2023

The History Press
97 St George's Place, Cheltenham,
Gloucestershire, GL50 3QB
www.thehistorypress.co.uk

British Library Cataloguing in Publication Data.
A catalogue record for this book is available from the British Library.

ISBN 978 1 80399 406 2

Typesetting and origination by The History Press
Printed and bound in Great Britain by TJ Books Limited, Padstow, Cornwall.

Public Records Office (1973) *Problems of a Growing City 1780–1870* (also various pamphlets).
Rodgers, N. (2000) *Equiano and Anti-Slavery in Eighteenth-century Belfast*, Ulster Historical Foundation.
Strain, R.W.M. (1961) *Belfast and Its Charitable Societies*, Oxford University Press.
Sweetman, R. & Nimmons, C. (1985) *Port of Belfast: 1785–1985*, Belfast Harbour Commissioners.
Townsend, Brian (1997) *The Last Distilleries of Ireland*, Neil Wilson Publishing.
Walker, B. (1983) *No Mean City*, Friar's Bush Press.
Walker, Brian M. (1994) *Shadows on Glass*, Appletree Press.

MAGAZINES

Various Copies of the *Belfast Magazine*, Glenravel History Project, Issues: 5, 9, 11, 30, 60, 72.
Rosemary Street Pulpit, Vol.47, No.6 (2009).

OTHER SOURCES

The Dublin University Calendar, Vol.3 (1912/13).

CONTENTS

ACKNOWLEDGEMENTS

The following people were very supportive in producing this book – Beth Amphlett, Jackie Chalk, Henry McDonald, Rudy Angus Stewart, Des Regan, Brenda Russell and especially Karen Scott.

All illustrations by Raymond O'Regan and Frankie Quinn.

INTRODUCTION

The Duke of Wellington, Samuel Beckett, C.S. Lewis, Jonathan Swift and Stalin's Foreign Minister: these are just a few of those people who played a part in shaping Belfast's history. As you weave your way through this *Little Book of Belfast*, it will highlight the depth of history in a city that began life in medieval times as a simple river crossing with few inhabitants.

Belfast has had its share of troubles through the many centuries of its existence. It has seen many challenges and triumphs, which will be laid out in the many stories here that trace its history; stories that will hopefully capture the spirit of this great city through its people, education, industry, charity, music, politics and so on.

As an example of the growth of Belfast, a population survey in 1801 showed Belfast with a population of 20,000 and Dublin with 200,000. By 1901 the figures were Belfast 349,000 and Dublin 348,000, and in the chapter on Belfast as an industrial giant you will see how this massive growth was achieved.

In the field of charity, Belfast opened the first fever hospital in Ireland in the 1790s, part of the ongoing efforts of the Belfast Charitable Society that was founded in 1752 and was responsible for providing an early form of free health care for the poor. All the doctors involved provided their services at no charge to their patients. An example of this was the lying-in hospital (a maternity hospital), which was opened in a house at 25 Donegall Street in 1785 to provide a safe environment for poor women to give birth in. The Belfast Charitable Society also opened a poor house in 1774 in North Queen Street to provide accommodation for the aged poor of the town. Again the physicians who attended the sick in the house gave of their services free.

This book tells Belfast's story from its foundation to the present day when it has become one of the 'must see' cities on the planet, voted one of the world's top destinations by *National Geographic*. It is a city that is alive with creativity, innovation, music, talent, craic, the odd drink and plenty of good humour. There is always something happening in Belfast with festivals throughout the year and world-class visitor attractions such as Titanic Belfast. What makes Belfast special are the people. What makes Belfast surprising are some of the hidden stories that its people have produced. Our aim is to give you a flavour of a unique and wonderful place.

1

ASPECTS OF BELFAST'S HISTORY

There is archaeological evidence of life in Belfast during the Neolithic period (4000–2500 BC), the Bronze Age (2500–500 BC) and the Iron Age (500 BC–AD 500). As just two examples of pre-historic structures, there is the Iron Age Giant's Ring on the outskirts of Belfast, which dates back to the Neolithic period and measures 200 metres across with five standing stones surrounding a megalithic chamber in the centre of an earthwork, and McArt's Fort, that famous prominence that stands out against the skyline of the Cavehill.

AD 82: Although the Romans never invaded Ireland, Cnaeus Julius Agricola, Governor of Britain had plans to cross over from Stranraer and enter the country by way of Belfast Lough, at that time known as Loch Lao – the Lough of the Calves.

150: Claudius Ptolemy, a Greco-Roman living in Alexandria, produced a map that included the eastern part of Ireland and which showed the river Logia, the Latin name for the river Lagan.

667: A battle took place between two of the warring tribes – the Ulidians and the Cruithins (Picts). This was when the name of Beal Feirste, which means 'the approach to the sandbank or ford', was first recorded. It was anglicised later and has today become Belfast.

1177: The Norman knight John de Courcy arrived in Belfast and built a motte and bailey on the banks of the river Farset just above the strategic crossing point between upper and lower Clandeboye. He later moved onto Carrickfergus where he built a more substantial castle, which remains to this day as a monument to him. At this time Loch Lao was known as Carrickfergus Lough, as Belfast was still only a very small settlement.

1210: King John passed through Belfast on his way to Carrickfergus.

1306: A tax roll of this year records the Little Church of the Ford, which was on the site of today's St George's in High Street and had a history that went all the way back to the tenth century.

Shankill Road has a history stretching all the way back even further, to the seventh century. The White Church that existed in this area was the Mother Church of Belfast, dating from this period to the sixteenth-century Reformation. This road was the ancient route out of Belfast to Antrim, 20 miles away, and over the nearby hills. In the 1830s a more direct route, the new Antrim Road, was built and the original Antrim Road was renamed Seanchill, which is Irish for 'old church' and was an acknowledgement of its former history.

1476: A more substantial Norman-type castle was built in Belfast on the site of today's British Home Stores. It was taken and demolished by one of the clan of the Clandeboye O'Neills.

1489/1503/1512/1523: The castle was taken and retaken by Hugh Roe O'Donnell in 1489 and then by the Earl of Kildare in 1503 and 1512. In 1523 the earl wrote to King Henry VIII that he had 'taken a castle of Hugh O'Neill's called Belfast and burned 24 miles of his country'.

1571: Belfast Castle and town were granted to Sir Thomas Smith.

1573: Belfast town was granted to the Earl of Essex.

1574: The Gaelic Lord Clandeboye O'Neill, his father and his wife, were arrested by Essex and sent to Dublin for execution.

1594–1603: Queen Elizabeth was determined to crush the last vestiges of the Ulster Gaels' resistance in Ireland, and they were eventually defeated in March 1603. It is ironic that shortly before the final defeat of the Ulster Gaels, in the Nine Years War, the queen died and King James VI of Scotland took over the crown to become King James I of England.

1603: Sir Arthur Chichester, a soldier from Devon, who fought in the Nine Years War, was rewarded for his efforts and granted Belfast and Upper and Lower Clandeboye (today's South Antrim and North Down), as well as other lands throughout Ulster. Initially he did not think too highly of Belfast and wrote, 'And albeit when I have it att best perfection I will gladly sell the whole landes for the ——— five poundes'.

Chichester would later change his mind and even turned down an opportunity to go to Virginia in America.

1605: Sir Arthur Chichester was appointed Lord Deputy of Ireland and he and King James began a plantation scheme for Ulster, whereby lowland Scottish Presbyterians and Anglicans from Devon were encouraged to come to Ulster with the promise of land. They also rewarded other soldiers who had fought in Queen Elizabeth's Nine Years War and were known as 'Undertakers'. These soldiers were granted 2,000 acres with the undertaking that they had to build English-style houses and a bawn – a protective wall, behind which the planters could retreat when under attack from the native Irish.

1605–16: Sir Arthur Chichester as Lord Deputy of Ireland – the King's Representative – was able during his tenure to add the Irish harp to the Royal Standard.

1611: Sir Arthur Chichester rebuilt Belfast Castle and in 1612 he was created Baron Chichester of Belfast.

1613: Belfast was granted borough status, which entitled it to send two MPs to the Dublin Parliament. Its first two MPs were Sir John Blennerhasset and George Trevillian. A borough allowed Belfast to have a sovereign (mayor), twelve burgesses, and freemen.

1625: Sir Arthur Chichester died and was buried alongside his wife in St Nicholas' Parish Church in Carrickfergus.

1636: The *Eagle's Wing*, a ship built in Belfast by Presbyterian ministers, set sail for New England but due to severe weather had to return home. It would not be until the 1750s that there would be a mass emigration of Presbyterians to America.

1642: A wall (rampier) was built around Belfast to protect the Scottish and English planters, as there was an uprising throughout Ireland by the native and Anglo-Irish Catholics.

1649: During the Cromwellian Period, Ireland supported King Charles I. A Colonel Venables marched to 'Royalist' Belfast and after a four-day siege he captured the town.

In 1644 the Belfast Presbyterians had taken over the Anglican Church in High Street but in 1649 Colonel Venables banished them not only from the church but from Belfast itself and turned the church into a citadel (fort), using lead from the roof to make musket bullets. The Presbyterian ministers would not be able to return to Belfast until the restoration of the monarchy under King Charles II, and even then it was not until around 1680 they were able to build their first meeting house in Hercules Street, today's Royal Avenue.

1688: The Long Bridge and its twenty-one arches, spanning the river Lagan was opened. The Earl of Donegall opened a Latin school at the corner of Ann Street and School House Lane (today's Church Lane). Also in this period the earl diverted the wide river Blackstaff (Owen Na Varra – the 'River of the Stakes') to emerge at what is today's Old Gasworks site at Cromac Street/Ormeau Road.

1690: King William III arrived in Ireland with his troops and stopped off in Belfast, staying in the castle of the Earl of Donegall's, who was the late Sir Arthur Chichester's nephew. The king was on his way to the Battle of the Boyne. The consequences of the defeat of King James II at the Battle of the Boyne, and the later Treaty of Limerick, would lead to the Dublin Parliament introducing the Penal Laws.

In the 1690s, sections of the Penal Laws, which in the main were directed against Catholics, would also affect Ulster Presbyterians, and in the eighteenth century this led to a strange alliance between radical Presbyterians and the native Irish Catholics, eventually leading to the 1798 uprising.

1695: The First Presbyterian Church was opened in Rosemary Street by Revd John McBride. He, like many Irish Presbyterians of his day, travelled to Glasgow to study for the ministry. In 1680 he was ordained Minister of Clare, County Armagh. By 1688 he had moved to Borgue near Kirkcudbright in Scotland. He returned to Ireland and was installed in Belfast in October 1694. At the time, the First Presbyterian Meeting House was at the corner of Hercules Lean, today's Royal Avenue. Reverend McBride was well known to the Earl of Donegall's family and used this connection to obtain a lease of land in Rosemary Lean where, in 1695, he opened a meeting house.

During the period of Queen Anne's reign (1702–14) the Dissenters were subjected to some of the Penal Laws that were mainly directed against the Catholic population. Some of the Penal Laws that applied to Presbyterians were that one could not attend Trinity College Dublin, be an officer in the army, become a member of a corporation (town council), or be a lawyer. The Presbyterian Sovereign (Mayor) of Belfast, David Buttle, had to leave office in July 1704 as he refused to take communion in the Church of Ireland church. One of the other Penal

Laws that applied to the Presbyterians was the payment of tithes (land taxes) to the Church of Ireland.

Another law mandated that anyone holding public office had to take an oath that the Pretender was not the son of James II. Reverend McBride refused to do this and fled to Scotland in 1705 to avoid arrest, returning in 1708. In 1709, McBride again refused to sign the Oath of Abjuration, and was due to be arrested. Having received this information in advance he fled once again to Scotland. As he made his escape over the Long Bridge, the site of today's Queen's Bridge, he was challenged by a sentry who recognised him and should have arrested him. Fortunately, the sentry was a member of Revd McBride's church and allowed him to continue his journey. McBride hid in a field in Ballymacaratt before making his way to Donaghadee Harbour and a boat to Scotland. While hiding in the field he lost a valuable gold ring belonging to the church which has never been found.

Back at the church in Rosemary Street, Sovereign Roger Haddock arrived to arrest the now absent McBride. After searching the church without success, he entered the manse next to the church and made his way to McBride's bedroom. Realising he had fled, in his frustration the Sovereign drew his sword and stabbed a portrait of McBride hanging over the bed. Today that damaged painting hangs in the Session Room of the First Presbyterian Church in Rosemary Street.

On the day of Queen Anne's death, Sunday 1 August 1714, a Schism Act came into effect in Ireland, which allowed the authorities to close down Presbyterian meeting houses. Queen Anne's death and the arrival of George I, the first king of the Hanoverian period, was welcome news to Irish Presbyterians.

An incident at the time sums up the dramatic change that took place. Robert McBride, son of Revd McBride, on hearing about Queen Anne's demise, mounted his father's old horse to spread the good news. On his journey he was stopped by a Church of Ireland minister. The encounter is recorded as follows: 'Hey, youngster, I suppose you and your mare are Presbyterian: She is so lean and meagre, and her ears hanging down, and you much in the same puritanical plight. Though I pity you, you deserve what you have got.' The boy replied,

'I thank you sir, but my mare will prick up her ears anon, and fling at all rough riders, since we know that Queen Anne is dead.' The churchman was aghast at the news and quickly scurried away.

The death of Queen Anne allowed the safe return of Revd McBride to Belfast where he continued as minister of the First Presbyterian Church in Rosemary Street until his death in 1718.

McBride's grandson, Admiral John McBride, escorted Princess Caroline to England in 1760 to marry George III. The famous American writer Edgar Allan Poe was also a descendent of McBride.

1701: Sovereign George McCartney was able to boast that Belfast was made up of 3,000 Presbyterians, 2,000 Episcopalians (Anglicans) and only 5 Papists.

Patrick Neill, from Scotland, who was invited over to Belfast in the 1690s, printed his first book, *A Book of Psalms*, followed in 1704 by his partner James Blow, who is credited with printing the first edition of the Bible in Ireland. There is some doubt about this claim as there is a record of him not printing his Bible until later.

1703: Arthur Chichester, the 3rd Earl of Donegall, set up a regiment in the grounds of his Belfast Castle, a regiment that later became the Royal Sussex Regiment.

1706: The 3rd Earl of Donegall, fighting with the Duke of Marlboro's forces in Spain, was killed at Fort Monjuich. He was buried in Spain. He had also been involved in the treaty that gave Gibraltar to Queen Anne.

1708: To add to the misery of the Earl of Donegall's family, their castle was severely damaged in a fire in which three of the Donegall children, along with a servant and the daughter of a minister, were lost. There were plans to rebuild the castle but it was decided instead that the family would move to England and become absentee landlords. Belfast and many other parts of Ireland were part of the Donegall family estate and agents would act for them in the collection of rent. Meanwhile, to cater for the increasing Presbyterian population, the Second Presbyterian Church was opened by Doctor Kirkpatrick, assistant to Revd McBride, directly behind the first church in Rosemary Street.

1732: It was recorded that the population of Belfast was 4,532 Protestant families and 340 Catholic families.

1737: Francis Joy, a Huguenot (French Protestant) founded the *Belfast News Letter and General Advertiser* at the Sign of the Peacock in Bridge Street, a paper that is still printed today, making it the oldest English-language paper still in production in the world.

1752: Belfast's first bank was opened and in the same year the Belfast Charitable Society was formed at the George Tavern.

1769: The absentee landlord, the 5th Earl of Donegall, laid the foundation stone of the Exchange Building in Waring Street. It was built to celebrate the birth of his son Augustus.

1770s: The Farset river, also known as the Belfast river, was covered over as far as the Corporation Church in High Street, which had fallen into a bad state of repair and was demolished and replaced by St Anne's Church in the newly opened Donegall Street.

1773: The height of Presbyterian emigration to America was reached, because of their treatment by the Anglican-dominated Dublin Parliament. It is estimated that in a twenty-year period around 200,000 Presbyterians emigrated from all over Ulster to America.

1774: The Belfast Charitable Society opened its poor house.

1778: The regular troops left Ireland to fight on behalf of the king in the American War of Independence and were replaced by local volunteers. John Paul Jones captured a British ship, the *Drake*, in Belfast Lough, which was considered to be the first naval victory in the American War of Independence.

1783: A newly built First Presbyterian Church was opened in Rosemary Street – the two previous churches dated back to 1695 and 1717.

1784: St Mary's Catholic Church was opened in Crooked Lane/Chapel Lane. The majority of the finance to build this church came from the Protestant community of Belfast. This was the first Catholic church to be opened in Belfast since the Reformation in the sixteenth century. As Father O'Hanlon entered the church to say the first mass, he passed a guard of honour laid on by the Belfast Company of Volunteers (all Protestants).

1785: Reverend Dr Crombie, minister of the First Presbyterian Church in Rosemary Street, opened what was referred to as 'the Academy' in the street that still bears its name. It would later move to the Cliftonville Road where it remains to this day as the Belfast Royal Academy. Reverend Crombie and the architect Lanyon were responsible for the beautiful elliptical church opened in 1783.

1786: The third edition of Robert Burns' poems was published in Belfast.

1787: The 'Bank of the Four Johns' was opened in Castle Place (all the founders had the same Christian name). A Methodist chapel was opened in Fountain Street, then called Water Street.

The following stories highlight Belfast's radical citizens and their attitude to the corrupt Dublin Parliament of the late eighteenth century, the actions of which in the end led to the failed 1798 Rebellion throughout Ireland and to the Act of Union in 1801.

DR WILLIAM DRENNAN (1754-1820)

Dr Drennan, one of the many eighteenth-century Belfast radicals, was born on 3 May 1754, the son of Revd Thomas and Anne Drennan. His father was minister of the First Presbyterian Church on Rosemary Street, and William was born in the manse next door to the church. He received his early education in Belfast before attending Glasgow University, where he obtained a Master of Arts in 1769. In 1773 he moved to Edinburgh to attend university there, leaving for Belfast in 1778 with a Doctorate in Medicine. Whilst living in both cities Drennan wrote and received many letters from his sister, mother and brother-in-law.

Drennan practised in Belfast up to 1783 and then moved to Newry, where he stayed until 1791, before moving to Dublin. Many of the letters Drennan wrote and received, which are estimated to number 1,400, dealt with the dire situation in Ireland, though one letter that Drennan wrote to his mother from Newry shows him in a lighter vein:

> A curious accident happened to me. I went to bed, fell asleep and was awakened with a burst of heat on the top of my head and starting up I tore off my head burnt out of both night-caps and yet the bed, curtain, sheets, etc., uninjured; all except the pillow which I lay on. I could have sworn that something had been put in my night-cap but the real truth was that in stooping to unbuckle my shoe I had popped the tassel

> of the caps into the candle which was placed on the chair and after going to bed it had burned into tinder on my head, the cotton not flaring. (*Drennan Letters*, No. 77A, *c*. 1783, Sept. 27th Newry)

While in Dublin Drennan continued to keep up the correspondence with his home town of Belfast, most of them to his sister Martha (Matty) McTier until his return to Belfast around 1807. In one of his many letters sent to Belfast, to his brother-in-law Samuel McTier on 21 May 1791, he sets out his thoughts for a brotherhood of Catholics, Protestants and Dissenters, which led to the formation of the Society of United Irishmen in Belfast at the Crown Tavern, Crown Entry, in October 1791. The Dublin branch of the United Irishmen was not set up until November 1791.

There is no mention of Drennan being actively involved in the 1798 uprising. Many believe his day in court in 1794 on sedition charges, and the death of his brother-in-law Samuel McTier, made him more cautious in his public pronouncements although still privately supporting the aims of the United Irishmen.

The failed 1798 uprising gave an impetus to those politicians who were behind the move to unite Ireland with Great Britain. In 1800 Drennan married Sarah Swanwick of Wem, Shropshire. She would bear him four sons and it is interesting to note the change in attitude of Belfast's radical Presbyterians when, in 1811, Drennan, now back in Belfast as editor (since 1808) of the *Belfast Monthly Magazine* wrote: 'Be Britons with all your souls ... and forget that your father called himself an Irishman' (*Belfast Monthly Magazine*, No. 41, Vol. 7, 31 December 1811). In the same article he also continued to rally support for Catholic emancipation, something that was promised when the Act of Union came into force in 1801. It caused the resignation of Pitt and Castlereagh from government when King George III vetoed the legislation.

THE PATRIOT, SAMUEL NEILSON (1761-1803)

Here was a man who was connected with most of the important events during the short existence of the United Irishmen (1791–1803) but is almost now a forgotten patriot.

Samuel Neilson was born in September 1761 at Ballyroney, County Down. His father, Alexander Neilson, was a dissenting minister. He received a liberal education, excelling in maths. He was also noted for his desire for knowledge. He entered the woollen-drapery trade, serving his apprenticeship, at age 16, in his brother's shop – John Neilson's Drapers Belfast.

In 1785 he married Nancy Bryson, the daughter of William Bryson, a wealthy Belfast merchant. Shortly after his marriage he set up his own business in Waring Street on the site of present-day Northern Whig. It was known as the Irish Woollen Warehouse. By 1792, the business had grown and he then owned property estimated at £8,000.

Samuel Neilson, along with other Belfast Presbyterian merchants, found his interest in politics when he joined the Belfast Volunteers. They were founded across Ireland on 17 March 1778 when regular troops left for America. The Volunteers were not under government control, which was a situation that the government would come to regret later. Many of the Belfast Volunteers would become members of the Society of United Irishmen when it was formed in October 1791. The society decided to publish its own newspaper, the *Northern Star*.

After the failure of the 1798 uprising, Samuel Neilson and ninety other United Irishmen were deemed too dangerous to be allowed to remain in Ireland, and a decision was taken either to exile or to transport them under the Banishment Act. The American President Adams, at the time, refused to accept any of the ninety United Irish prisoners. In 1799 Samuel Neilson along with Revd Sinclair Kelburn, William Tennant and Thomas Russell were shipped off to Fort George in Scotland. Samuel Neilson was not released until June 1802 and was forbidden under pain of execution to return home to Belfast.

After a clandestine return via Dublin to Belfast to say farewell to his family he left for America. Tragically he died within a year of arriving and is buried in Poughkeepsie, New York State.

The Northern Star *Newspaper*

In 1792 Samuel Neilson was the main mover in setting up the *Northern Star* newspaper, published in Wilsons Court just off High Street. The aims of the paper were stated as 'Parliamentary reform, founded on a real representation of the people and also to the union of the people of all religious persuasions'.

The first edition of the *Northern Star* was published on 14 January 1792. Samuel Neilson was the editor and with his enthusiasm and zeal the paper achieved a circulation during its life of 4,000–5,000 copies. The paper was accepted by the authorities as the mouthpiece of the United Irishmen and so when Britain declared war with France in 1793 it came under greater scrutiny.

The main contributors to the *Northern Star* included three Presbyterian ministers: reverends Porter, Kelburn and Steel Dickson. Reverend Porter was the editor of the famous 'Billy Bluff and the Squire' articles. They were of satirical nature aimed at the Earl of Londonderry and his agent and spy Revd John Cleland. The unfortunate Revd Porter was to pay dearly for those articles. He was later tried by court martial and hanged in 1798 at Grey Abbey on ground between his home and his church. A plea by his wife for leniency was rejected by Lord Londonderry.

In 1795 Samuel Neilson became the sole proprietor and editor of the *Northern Star* when his other partners withdrew. In 1797, with Neilson in a Dublin prison, up to seventy members of the Monaghan Militia entered the premises of the *Northern Star* in Wilson's Court and damaged the printing presses beyond use.

The *Northern Star* had been published twice weekly from 1792 until 1797. There are some copies in the Belfast Central Library Newspaper Archive section.

THE UNITED IRISHMEN AND THEIR CONNECTION WITH THE BELFAST CHAMBER OF COMMERCE

The Belfast Chamber of Commerce was founded on 25 October 1783. It was formed to represent the business community but had an interesting and mainly hidden history relating to some of the activities of its members during the turbulent period leading up to the 1798 Rebellion.

In the second half of the eighteenth century, Belfast's merchants, mostly Presbyterians, held radical views on their lack of Parliamentary representation in the Dublin Parliament. This led many Presbyterian merchants to adopt the aspirations of the United Irish Society, founded in Belfast in October 1791. The following are just a small sample of Belfast Chamber of Commerce members who were also members or supporters of the United Irishmen.

John Boyle

Boyle was a partner with Waddell Cunningham in the import–export of French brandy (barilla). As with many of the future supporters of the United Irish cause, John Boyle first joined the Belfast Company of Volunteers when it was formed in March 1778. The Volunteers were formed to fill the gap when regular troops were drafted to America during the War of Independence. John Boyle was also one of the original twelve proprietors of the United Irish newspaper, the *Northern Star*.

Hugh Crawford, originally from Ballymena, had a shop in North Street, Belfast, before moving into the linen trade and later into sugar refining. He was a member of the Third Presbyterian Church in Rosemary Street along with the famous and tragic United Irishman Henry Joy McCracken. He joined the Belfast Volunteers in 1778 and like many others became a member of the United Society when it was formed in 1791.

In 1793 the Volunteers were disbanded. Some who were also members of the United Irish Society left that organisation, though Hugh Crawford remained a member. Crawford belonged to a small, secret cell of the United Irish Society run by the bookseller John Hughes. In October 1797, John Hughes was arrested and after the failure of the 1798 Rebellion his fellow church member Henry Joy McCracken was hanged for his part in the rebellion.

Robert Getty

Getty was a merchant, trading in tea, flax seed, tobacco, Dutch starch and French brandy. He was also a member of the Belfast General Insurance Company. Getty was a radical campaigner for Catholic emancipation and issued a statement in 1792 as follows: 'We anxiously wish to see the day when every Irishman shall be a citizen ... when Catholics and Protestants ... equal freedom, equal privileges ... shall look on each other as brothers ... natives of the same land.' Although Robert Getty had very radical views, he did not take an active part in the 1798 uprising. However, he was arrested in June 1798 as two cannons under his care when he was in the Volunteers had gone missing without his knowledge. It is believed that he was betrayed and framed by the United Irishman, turned informer, James McGucken. Robert Getty survived the troubled 1798 Rebellion and with others such as Dr Drennan and John Lawless he continued to push for Catholic emancipation and the dismantling of the remainder of the Penal Laws.

Henry Haslett

Originally from Limavady, Henry Haslett set up business as a woollen draper in Rosemary Street, Belfast. In the 1790s he was involved in shipping, insurance and imports and was part of a shipping syndicate called the New Traders. The syndicate gave William Ritchie's shipyard its first order, one of three ordered by the syndicate, with the other two named the *Shamrock* and the *St Patrick*. It is not a surprise that the ships all had Irish names as virtually all of the members of the New Traders were sympathetic to or members of the United Irish Society. Haslett was one of the original members who set up the United Irish Society at the Crown Tavern in October 1791. He was also one of the twelve original proprietors of the United Irish newspaper, the *Northern Star*. Even after the Volunteers were proscribed and disbanded in 1793 he remained and got more deeply involved as the United Irish Society became an underground movement. In 1796 he, along with seven other United Irishmen, were arrested on charges of high treason. He was held for fourteen months in Kilmainham Jail in Dublin and not released until December 1797. While he was in jail two of his children died, and to add to his distress his 23-year-old sister also died while on a visit to see him in Dublin.

Henry Haslett died in 1806 and was buried at Knockbreda Cemetery, Belfast. The oration was given by his fellow United Irishman, the famous Revd Dr Steele Dickson.

It is significant that all the United Irishmen in Belfast and Ulster were Presbyterian. They had strong differences of opinion as to the Catholic Church's teaching but their idea was a coming together of what Dr William Drennan called a 'Brotherhood of Catholic, Protestant and Dissenter'.

ISABELLA 'BELLE' MARTIN – IRELAND'S MATA HARI

Belle Martin was born into a very poor family in Portaferry in around 1767. She had grown up under the eye of Revd Dickson, who referred to himself as 'her guardian' and to her as 'with a handsome face' that 'exposed her to temptations, to resist which she proved deficient, either in wisdom or in will'.

Belle Martin's move to Belfast eventually brought her into contact with government agents, like Edward Newell, who reported to Colonel Barber and who also had a close relationship with Edward Cooke in Dublin Castle, and she managed to get a job in the Benjamin Franklin Tavern in Sugarhouse Entry, owned by the Barclay Family, which was used as a meeting place for the United Irishmen.

When the United Irishmen met they used the cover name of the Muddlers Club. Belle Martin in her role as a spy was passing information she gleaned from the Muddlers Club meetings back to the authorities. She would also go out at night (there is some evidence that she had first travelled to Belfast as a prostitute). She would entrap off-duty soldiers and citizens by falsely persuading them to join the United Irish Society. She had soldiers in wait ready to arrest any man who would succumb to her charms.

In 1796 Belle Martin moved to Dublin, probably on the orders of Lord Castlereagh and due to her services as a government spy. Her reputation followed her. In Dublin, Watty Cox produced an undercover news sheet called the *Union Star* in which he published descriptions of people he accused of being government agents. In 1797 he warned any United Irishman to be wary of having any dealings with the brewer, Arthur Guinness. Belle Martin was also included in one of his lists. Cox gave a description of her: about 30 years old, yellowish hair (this was a reference to her blonde hair), lady of the night, strong Northern accent. So she was obviously well known to her enemies. While in Dublin she lived at Dublin Castle, Pembroke Street and Bridewell Barracks. On page 5 of 'Account of Secret Service Money in Ireland 1797' there are two entries referring to Belle Martin:

> 1797 – 1st November – Keeper of Bridewell for Bell Martin Diet 21 weeks £12.16.10½d
> 1797 – 3rd November – Bell Martin to take her out of town, etc. £5.13.9d

Yet even with her notorious reputation as a spy, Belle Martin was able to get the position of housekeeper to William Aylmer, a prominent United Irishman in Painstown, Kildare.

There are many different versions of her Christian name: Belle, Bell, Isabella and even Elizabeth. In one report to Dublin Castle she is referred to as Isabella 'Belle' Martin and is described as 'a servant girl who was responsible for the arrest of many United Irishmen in Belfast'.

She, along with other informers, received payments for their services; these were sometimes substantial. The highest single payment to any informer was £1,000 to Frances Higgins for information leading to the arrest of Lord Edward Fitzgerald. The arrest was carried out by Major Henry Sirr, who was based in Dublin Castle and co-ordinated security policy against the United Irishmen and arrested many of them. The proof of Higgins' deed is shown in the Secret Service accounts as 'F.H. Discovery of L.E.F. £1,000'. Higgins was editor of the *Freeman's Journal* and used his staff to spy on United Irish activities.

We know that in 1797 Belle Martin was living at Pembroke Street but there is no evidence of her place of abode after the failure of the 1798 Rebellion. It is doubtful, with her reputation, that she moved back to Belfast.

BELFAST AFTER THE FAILED 1798 REBELLION

By late summer of 1798 the United Irish had been defeated. Although Belfast was still under military rule anybody found with a pike, which was the weapon used by most of the United Irishmen, would be arrested and brought in for trial. General Nugent made each householder in the town post a list of residents on the outside of each dwelling. If any were absent from sunset to sunrise the owner would be court-martialled. To add to the misery, the years of 1799 and early 1800 brought a period of erratic and unusual weather conditions. This raised the spectre of famine as many of the crops were destroyed.

The Act of Union, which came into effect on 1 January 1801, was eventually accepted by the majority of Belfast people and the 1798 Rebellion was consigned to the long and turbulent history of Belfast, though even then there were other attempted uprisings, as in 1803: Robert Emmet's failed uprising in Dublin and Thomas Russell's equally failed uprising in the North. Both were hanged; Emmet in Dublin, and his head cut off, and Russell, his head also cut off, and buried in Downpatrick.

1809: A house of industry was opened in Marquis Street, just off Smithfield Square. It was set up to give work to the poor. A new toll bridge was erected over the river Lagan at Ormeau.

1810: The foundation stone of the Academical Institution was laid in this year. Designed by Sir John Soane, the architect who designed the Bank of England, the Institution was opened in 1814 and would be awarded the title of 'Royal' in the 1830s. Notably, Soane provided his services free.

1811: The second Catholic church, St Patrick's, was completed in Belfast, again supported mainly by Protestant finance. It was officially opened in 1815. The original iron railings were the gift of Lord Londonderry.

1817: As had happened in other counties throughout Ireland, a fever hospital was opened in Frederick Street. At the same time a house of correction was opened in Howard Street. The *History of Belfast* was published, the author of which, Henry Joy, was part of the famous Joy–McCracken dynasty.

1823: The opening of Belfast Gas Works brought light to the town.

1824: The first edition of the *Northern Whig* newspaper was published by Francis Dalzell Finlay.

1825: Michael Andrews, originally from Comber, opened a damask factory at Ardoyne (in Irish, Ard Eoin – Owens Height).

1828: May Street Presbyterian Church was opened to give the Revd Henry Cooke a platform in Belfast for his Orthodox Presbyterian views.

1832: There were outbreaks of typhus, cholera and influenza.

1839: The Ulster Railway opened and ran services from Belfast to Lisburn (the first railway service in Ulster).

1839–41: There was another outbreak of cholera in Belfast.

1841: The Government opened up workhouses throughout Ireland with one in Belfast on the Lisburn Road, the site of the present-day City Hospital.

1843: The new Queen's Bridge was opened. It replaced the famous 1688 Long Bridge of twenty-one arches. A deaf-and-dumb institution was opened in Donegall Street Congregational Church.

1845: Crumlin Road Jail, designed by Lanyon, was opened, followed shortly afterwards by Crumlin Road Court House directly opposite and with a connecting tunnel for the secure movement of prisoners back and forth.

1847: The emigrant ship, the *Swatara,* attempting to reach America was forced to return and landed in Belfast, leading to an outbreak of typhus in the town.

1849: Queen Victoria and Prince Albert visited. Queen's College was opened; it was one of three non-denominational colleges in Ireland, the other two being in Galway and Cork.

1851: Belfast's population increased to over 100,000. The Great Famine 1845–51 affected Belfast with the recently opened workhouses unable to cope, leading to many deaths from disease.

1853: The Presbyterian College opened in Botanic Avenue. The young Earl of Belfast, Frederick Richard Chichester, died of scarlet fever in Naples and his mother brought his body back to be buried in Belfast.

1855: A statue in memory of the Earl of Belfast was erected in front of the Royal Belfast Academical Institute (known as Inst).

1858: The straightening of the Channel out of Belfast Harbour allowed the slob land to be dumped on the east side of the river Lagan; it was called Dargan's Island, after the engineer William Dargan. Its name was changed to Queen's Island and this is where iron ship building was established under the ownership of Hickson & Co., who had an iron foundry in Cromac Street and needed an outlet for their products. Edward Harland, from Yorkshire, was brought in to manage the yard. Harland eventually bought Hickson's shipbuilding company and he in turn brought Gustav Wolff over from England, and the shipyard soon afterwards became known as Harland and Wolff.

1862: The Ulster Hall in Bedford Street was opened.

1864: There were sectarian riots in Belfast. The Royal Irish Constabulary took over policing from the local Belfast police force.

1865: The Methodist College was founded on the Malone Road.

1866: Charles Lanyon, the architect, was elected as a Belfast MP to sit in the House of Commons, London.

1869: The Albert Clock, to commemorate the death of Prince Albert, was completed, but due to the glacial land it was built on it eventually developed a lean of at least 3 feet.

1871: A new Town Hall was opened in Victoria Street – it would only last until the opening of the grand City Hall in 1906.

1872: Horse-drawn trams were introduced into Belfast.

1876: The statue of Revd Henry Cooke replaced the original statue of the young Earl of Belfast outside the gates of the Royal Belfast Academical Institute ('Inst'). It is said the statue was deliberately positioned so as not to face into Inst as he objected to its liberal Presbyterian views. However, the original statue of the young earl, known as 'The Black Man', also had its back to the college, even though he was a friend of Inst. His statue, still all in black, now rests in the City Hall.

1877: The original 1815 St Patrick's Catholic Church in Donegall Street was replaced by the more Gothic church which survives to the present day.

1879: The Workman Clarke Shipyard was opened, and would in time equal the success of its older neighbour, Harland and Wolff.

1881: Up to 4,000 people, many of them butchers, were moved from the small and narrow Hercules Street to make way for the rather grand Royal Avenue.

1883: The last of the male line of the Chichester family, the 3rd Marquis, died and what was left of the estate went to Harriet Chichester, who had married Anthony Ashley Cooper. He would later become the 9th Earl of Shaftsbury, and it was Shaftsbury money that completed the building of Belfast Castle on the slopes of the Cavehill. In the mid-nineteenth century most of the Donegall leases in Belfast (about 700) had been sold off under the Encumbered Estates Court to pay off debts owed by the Chichester–Donegall family.

1886: Albert Bridge collapsed. It was originally known as the 'Half Penny Bridge', because of the toll that had to be paid to cross it when it was first opened.

1888: Woodvale Park opened on the Woodvale Road. Robinson & Cleavers Royal Irish Linen store opened at the corner of Donegall Place. Belfast was awarded city status.

1889: On a visit to Belfast the future king, Prince Albert Victor, opened the Alexandra Graving docks and laid the foundation stone for the new Albert Bridge.

1890: The famous Nationalist MP Joseph Gillis Biggar died. He was renowned for using blocking tactics in the House of Commons, and had worked closely with the famous Nationalist MP Charles Stewart Parnell. He had a strong Belfast accent, described by some of his critics as 'rasping'. He would address the Speaker of the Commons as 'Muster Speaker'.

1890s: The White Linen Hall, opened in 1785, was demolished to make way for a new City Hall. The present-day Linen Hall Library, whose main entrance is at the corner of Donegall Square North and Fountain Street, still owes its name to its former home, the White Linen Hall.

1906: The magnificent City Hall was opened. It was designed by the 38-year-old Alfred Brumwell Thomas, who won the competition to build it against many more senior

architects. It was constructed of the best Portland stone with Italian and Greek marble used extensively in the interior. Alfred Brumwell Thomas was knighted for his design of the building.

1912: The Home Rule Crisis erupted and the Covenant was signed. The *Titanic* was launched from the Harland and Wolff Shipyard.

1914/18: The start of the First World War most likely prevented a civil war as both sides, the Unionist UVF and the Nationalist Volunteers, put their arguments aside until the defeat of the Germans. Two Belfast soldiers, William McFadzean, originally from Lurgan, and Frederick Hall both won the Victoria Cross for their actions in the 1914–18 war. Private McFadzean was killed during the Battle of the Somme in 1916 after throwing himself on top of a box of grenades when two of the safety pins had become free. He was killed outright but saved the lives of his comrades.

HMS *Caroline* is one of only three surviving warships from the First World War and is the last survivor of the Battle of Jutland. She is berthed in Alexandra Docks in Belfast.

1920: Ulster (six counties) was granted Home Rule.

1921: King George V opened the first parliament, held in the City Hall.

1922: Civil strife returned to Belfast. The new parliament was moved to the Presbyterian College in Botanic Avenue where it remained until the Stormont Parliament building was opened in 1932.

1939: 3 September. Germany invaded Poland leading to Britain declaring war.

1945: 4 May. Germany surrendered, ending the war in Europe, followed by the Japanese surrender in 1946. Leading Seaman James Maginnes, from Belfast, was awarded the Victoria Cross for his actions in 1945, along with Lt Ian Fraser in destroying the 10,000-ton Japanese cruiser the *Takao*; he was the only person from Northern Ireland to win this award in the Second World War.

1949: Northern Ireland's status within the United Kingdom was confirmed by the Labour Government as the Irish Free State had been declared a republic.

1951: There was a decline in the linen industry.

1956–62: The Official IRA began sporadic attacks, mostly around the border. The main reason put forward by them for ceasing their border campaign was that they were not getting support from the majority of the Northern Catholics.

1963: Lord Brookborough retired as Prime Minister of Northern Ireland and was replaced by Captain Terence O'Neill.

1968–69: A call for civil rights led to an outbreak of civil strife and the arrival of troops.

1990s: Various ceasefires led up to the 1998 Good Friday Agreement brokered by the former US Senator, George Mitchell. John Hume (Social Democratic Labour Party) and David Trimble (Ulster Unionist Party), who were both MPs and leaders of their respective parties, received the Nobel Peace Prize.

2014: The power-sharing government, with many changes in make-up operating.

2

FAMOUS PEOPLE AND THEIR CONNECTION TO BELFAST

Over the years Belfast has built up a real treasure chest of scientists, inventors, actors, musicians, war heroes, writers and many more universal names not normally associated with the city.

JOHN STEWART BELL (1929–90)

After finishing secondary school and Belfast Technical College, John Bell started work at Queen's University in the physics department as a laboratory assistant. After taking a degree in theoretical physics he moved to Trinity College Dublin and Birmingham University. He is best remembered for the Bell inequalities, which are an important part of quantum theory. He moved from atomic energy research in Harwell to the Cern Nuclear Centre in Geneva, where he died at the age of 62, after an illustrious life in the world of physics.

PRESIDENT CLINTON AND SENATOR GEORGE MITCHELL (PEACEMAKERS)

The Good Friday Agreement was signed in Belfast on Good Friday in 1998. It was a power-sharing agreement between the different political parties, and is still in operation in 2014. George Mitchell had been assigned to mediate by President Clinton, the first US President not only to visit Northern Ireland but to take an active interest in establishing a power-sharing agreement between the parties. George Mitchell should have been awarded the Nobel Peace Prize, along with John Hume (Nationalist) and David Trimble (Unionist), as there would not have been an agreement without his valiant efforts, diligence and diplomacy. At the front of the City Hall, just to the left of Queen Victoria's statue, is a memorial plaque set in the ground commemorating President Clinton's visit to the city. (It is just below the memorial to the Second World War landing of US troops in Belfast.)

JOHN BOYD DUNLOP (1840–1921)

Dunlop had a veterinary practice at 50 Gloucester Street in Belfast. On 28 February 1888 he had been working with his son's tricycle, and discovered that inflated tubes covered in canvas and held together with a rubber solution provided the base for a more comfortable and smoother ride. Later that same year Dunlop patented his invention of a pneumatic tyre (patent no. 10607). He was not the original inventor of the tyre but he was the first to apply the name pneumatic. W. Bolin & Co. made the frames for his new invention, which quickly caught on. Many cycle races were now using his tyres; one in particular was held during Queen's College Sports Day. Billy Hulme, won every race by a large margin. Dunlop sold his patent to Harvey Du Cros and eventually

moved to Dublin to work with the firm of Bowden & Gillies, who manufactured frames for the Dunlop tyres.

Dunlop died on 23 August 1921. In August 1990 the Northern Bank (now Danske Bank) issued a £10 note featuring Dunlop.

CHAIM HERZOG (1918–97)

Chaim Herzog's father was the rabbi of the Annesley Street Synagogue in Belfast and lived at 185 Cliftonpark Avenue in north Belfast. Chaim was born in 1918, before the family moved to Dublin, where his father had been appointed Chief Rabbi to Ireland. Then in 1935 the family moved to Palestine.

Chaim studied law in London and qualified as a barrister. When the war broke out he joined the British Army, first of all as a tank commander, before moving to military intelligence. By the time he left the army he had attained the rank of major. From 1947 he saw service in the newly formed State of Israel. His first post was as Head of Intelligence (IDF), and he then rose to the rank of general. He would also be involved in various public and political offices and in 1981 was appointed Israel's Ambassador to the United Nations. In 1983 he was elected President of Israel and held that office for two terms, 1983–93, the maximum allowed. Before his death in Tel Aviv on 17 April 1997 he made a return visit to Dublin and finally to his place of birth in Belfast. The house where Chaim was born, 185 Cliftonpark Avenue, has an Ulster History Circle plaque on the outside wall in memory of this 'Son of Belfast'.

HENRY GEORGE FERGUSON (1884–1960)

In 1911, Harry Ferguson began business in Belfast by opening a car showroom in May Street, later moving to larger premises in Donegall Square East. He began selling American tractors in 1914. He redesigned the coupling on the plough, giving it his famous three point linkage, and patented his design as the Ferguson System. By 1938 he had in informal agreement with Henry Ford and had become Ford's only partner.

Over 300,000 of the Ferguson System Ford tractors were built. When Henry Ford's grandson took over the Ford Motor Company he attempted, unsuccessfully, to disregard the agreement between his grandfather and Ferguson, but Ferguson won the law suit. He designed a new model, the 'Wee Fergie' model number TC-20, and these newly designed lightweight and inexpensive tractors were built by the Standard Motor Company in Coventry, eventually selling over 500,000. He formed a new company with a Canadian firm, and Massey Ferguson Tractors are still sold worldwide today.

Harry Ferguson is also famous for designing and building his own aeroplane, which he flew along the beach at Newcastle, County Down in 1909. This was only a short time after the Wright Brothers made their first flight!

MAXIM LITVINOV (1876–1951)

Maxim Litvinov taught in the Jaffe Public Elementary School on the Cliftonville Road. The school had been established by Belfast's Jewish community in 1907 and tragically burned down in 1997.

Litvinov was one of the many who left Russia during the pogroms against the Jews in the late nineteenth century, although he was originally of Polish descent. In 1917 he returned to take part in the Bolshevik Revolution. He worked his way through the ranks of the Communist Government and in the 1930s he became Stalin's Foreign Minister.

JAMES JOSEPH MAGENNIS (1910–66)

James Magennis was the only person from Northern Ireland to be awarded the Victoria Cross in the Second World War.

He was born and lived at 4 Majorca Street in the Grosvenor Road area of Belfast. He joined the Royal Navy, aged 16, in 1935 and after serving on several warships he was selected for service in the X Craft (mini-sub) Special Services. In July 1945 he was operating with his group in Australia and they attacked two Japanese warships the *Myoko* and *Takao*. Lt Ian Fraser and Leading Seaman James Magennis, under treacherous conditions, managed to sink the 10,000-ton *Takao* in their mini-sub. Both were awarded the Victoria Cross.

Despite being the only man from Northern Ireland to win a Victoria Cross he was denied the Freedom of the City, although he benefited from a fund of £3,000 collected by public subscription. As well as the snub from the city fathers, he also had to deal with being shunned by some of the Catholic community, and so in 1955 he and his family moved to Bradford, the home town of his wife Edna Skidmore. He died in 1986 and there is a memorial to him in his adopted home. Back in Belfast a 6-foot-high Portland and bronze memorial (shaped like a capstan) was unveiled in the grounds of the City Hall. It is just to the right of Queen Victoria's statue as you enter the front gates. There is also a portrait of James Magennis in the War Memorial Building in Talbot Street, Belfast.

WILLIAM FREDERICK MCFADZEAN (1896–1916)

William Frederick McFadzean was a posthumous winner of the Victoria Cross. He was born in Lurgan, but the family moved to Belfast, living at Number 372 Cregagh Road. He joined the 14th Battalion of the Royal Irish Rangers, and in the Battle of the Somme his duty was to go over the top carrying buckets of grenades. While he was waiting in the trenches on 1 July 1916, preparing for an attack near Thiepval Wood, a box of grenades fell into the bottom of the trench. Two of the safety pins were dislodged and McFadzean threw himself on top of the box, which exploded, killing him instantly though he saved the lives of the other soldiers. His father, William, received his son's posthumous Victoria Cross at Buckingham Palace in 1917. William Frederick McFadzean VC is remembered in Thiepval, Newtownbreda Presbyterian Church, Lurgan Presbyterian Church, at Collegians Rugby Club (for which he played) and in Castlereagh Borough Council.

SIR JAMES MURRAY (1788–1871)

James Murray was an apothecary in High Street, Belfast. He also worked for a period with the Belfast Dispensary and Fever Hospital in Frederick Street. He had been experimenting with liquid magnesium to settle stomach pains. When the Marquis of Anglesey, the Lord Lieutenant of Ireland, was on a visit north to see his friend, the 2nd Marquis of Donegall, he complained of an upset stomach. James Murray was called in and recommended his potion to the earl – to this day the potion is still known as Milk of Magnesia and is sold throughout the world. James Murray eventually moved to Dublin and for his services to the lord lieutenant he was knighted. James Murray has a street called Murray Terrace named after him, which runs along the side of RBAI and, contrary to popular belief, is not named because of his discovery, but because he owned a row of Georgian house in the street. When Sir James Murray died in 1871 he was buried in Dublin, although his two sons are buried in the famous Clifton Street Graveyard in Belfast.

FRANK PANTRIDGE (1916–2004)

Professor James Francis Pantridge was born in 1916. He attended two schools, one of which was the Friends School in Lisburn, before commencing a medical degree at Queen's University Belfast, graduating in 1939 just on the outbreak of the Second World War. It is interesting that while he was at Queen's one of his lecturers was Professor Theodore Thomson Flynn, Errol Flynn's father.

During the war, Pantridge served as a medical officer until his capture in 1942 when Singapore was taken by the Japanese. During his detention in Malaya and Tanbaya, the Burmese death camp, he provided invaluable medical assistance to prisoners, for which he was awarded the Military Cross. On this return to Belfast after the war he returned to the Royal Victoria Hospital where he established the cardiac department. With his work in the cardiac unit Frank Pantridge realised there was a problem in that by the time an ambulance arrived at a heart-attack incident the patient could already be dead.

Before 1965, the heart defibrillator was found only in medical centres and hospitals and was not available to ambulances. It was estimated that treatment of a heart attack within 30 minutes of its occurring could save the life of the patient. So, in 1965 Pantridge and Dr John Geddes modified the defibrillator in the hospital by the use of two car batteries and made it portable. It meant that the personnel in the world's first cardiac ambulance could deliver an electric shock to restart the patient's heart at the scene of the attack. This invention of, what would be called for a long time the Pantridge Defibrillator, saved thousands of lives throughout the world and today portable defibrillators almost everywhere, including large shopping malls.

Professor Frank Pantridge was awarded the CBE in 1979 for his work in cardiology and in particular for the Pantridge Defibrillator. He retired from the Royal Victoria Hospital in 1982.

SIR JOHN SOANE (1753–1837)

Sir John Soane, the designer of the Bank of England building, also designed the Royal Belfast Academical Institution, the foundation stone of which was laid in 1810. The original plan was for a building twice the size of what is seen today, but it had to be curtailed due to lack of finance. This need for finance also led to the lease of land for the building of the Belfast Technical College, opened in 1907, and which dominated one half of the great lawn that fronted the college.

WILLIAM THOMSON, LORD KELVIN (1824–1907)

William Thomson was born in 1824 at College Square East (a blue plaque on a modern, present-day building commemorates this). He was the son of Professor James Thomson, who taught mathematics in the nearby Belfast Academical Institution. In 1832 his family moved to Glasgow when his father was appointed Professor of Mathematics at Glasgow University. William was able to attend his father's university when only 11 years old before gaining a place at Peterhouse College in Cambridge. When he graduated from Peterhouse, he was invited to take up an appointment as Professor of Natural Philosophy at Glasgow University, aged only 22. He held this position until his retirement in 1899.

Kelvin is renowned for his work on mechanical energy and heat which led to the temperature scale that still carries his name to this day (on this scale the freezing point of water is at 273.15 kelvin).

His other inventions included a sensitive mirror galvanometer used in 1866 when a transatlantic telegraph cable was laid between Valencia Island, Ireland, to Trinity Bay in Newfoundland, Canada. He also invented a new compass which was used by the Royal Navy. He was honoured and made Baron Kelvin of Largs in 1892 for his

contribution to science. Kelvin died near Largs in 1907 and is buried in Westminster Abbey. His mother, who remarried in Belfast, is buried in Clifton Street Graveyard.

ERNEST WALTON (1903–95)

Although born in Dungarvan, County Waterford, Ernest Walton's family moved to Belfast and Walton attended Methodist College there from 1915 to 1922. He was head boy at the college and would later marry the head girl Freda Wilson. After leaving Methodist College he went to Trinity College Dublin. He later gained a place at Trinity College, Cambridge University, during which time he and John Cockcroft built a linear accelerator. This led to the famous splitting of the atom in 1932 for which they both received the Nobel Prize for Physics. After returning from Cambridge he moved back to Belfast in 1934. The college named its new science and technology building in his honour. One of his three daughters taught in Methodist College, thus preserving the link with the Walton name. Ernest Walton died on 25 June 1995.

ARTHUR WELLESLEY, THE DUKE OF WELLINGTON (1769–1852)

Did you ever wonder why there are so many references to the Duke of Wellington in Belfast, for example Wellington Place, Wellesley Avenue (Wellesley was the duke's surname) and Mornington Crescent? The duke's mother, Anne, the Countess Mornington, lived for a time in Belfast at Anna's Dale, which is the present-day Annadale and the site of Wellington College.

The young Wellesley began his military career at the age of 18, joining the 73rd Highlanders as an ensign. His mother did not have much confidence in his prospects, commenting, 'Arthur has put on his red coat for the first time today. Anyone can see he does not have the cut of a soldier.' To add insult to injury she followed this up with 'I vow to god I don't know what I shall do with my awkward son Arthur.' This was the man who went on to defeat Napoleon at Waterloo!

The late film stars Errol Flynn, James Mason, Stephen Boyd and some of the greats in literature, Swift, C.S. Lewis, Beckett and Trollop, all have a connection with Belfast and their stories are covered in more detail in Chapter 6.

3

BELFAST: AT ONE TIME AN INDUSTRIAL GIANT

Before its rise to become an industrial giant in the mid-nineteenth and early twentieth centuries, many small manufacturing industries thrived in Belfast, from the seventeenth through to the early nineteenth centuries. Below is a list of some of the industries mentioned in Belfast's records along with the date in which they were recorded.

TANNERIES (THIRTY-TWO IN TOTAL)

Waring Street 1670
High Street 1678 (Geo. Martin)
Smithfield Square North 1788
Barrack Street 1824
King Street 1824 (tannery and glue works)

POTTERY (FIVE IN TOTAL)

Hill Street 1698–1725. Wedgewood objected to this Belfast pottery, which had a short existence of only twenty-seven years. There are very few surviving examples of the Belfast pottery but there is a plaque, just off Hill Street, to commemorate its short existence.

SOAP AND TALLOW MANUFACTURERS (FORTY-ONE IN TOTAL)

Waring Street 1712
Peters Hill 1753

Alexander Finlay's Soap and Candle Works, Ann Street 1798
Pottinger's Entry 1801
Robert Linn & Co., High Street 1807/8

FOUNDRIES (SIXTY IN TOTAL) – A MIXTURE OF IRON, BRASS, COPPER AND TIN

Lagan Foundry 1799
Belfast Foundry, Dargan Street 1811
Union Street 1813

PAPER MANUFACTURERS

Cromac Mills 1749
Mr Blow's Mill 1777
Pottinger's Entry 1807 – Blow Ward & Co. The John Ward name will come up again in relation to the famous Belfast firm of Marcus Ward & Co. which set up business in 1802.
Henry Joy, Pottinger's Entry 1807
James Blow Jnr, Patrick Street 1824

SUGAR REFINING

Rosemary Street 1750 and 1773. It is interesting to note that the Rosemary Street sugarhouse was converted to cotton manufacturing in 1781.
Waring Street 1756 and 1813

GUN MANUFACTURERS (EIGHTEEN IN TOTAL)

William Pearce, Rosemary Street 1756
Robert McCormick, Arthur Street 1793
John McFarlane, Peters Hill 1813
Daniel Hamill, Berry Street 1839
James Nicholl, Waring Street 1839

DISTILLERIES (TEN IN TOTAL)

John McKelvey, Castle Street 1759
William Hopps, Church Lane 1761
Napiers Distillery, Bank Street 1792
Ann Street 1798
Tennent Street 1833
Emerson, Arbuthnot & Co., Arthur Place 1839

GLASS WORKS (SIX IN TOTAL)

Belfast Glass Manufacturing 1766 and 1781
Belfast Glass Works, Peters Hill 1803
Shamrock Glass Works, Short Strand 1823

TOBACCO MANUFACTURERS (THIRTY-SEVEN IN TOTAL – THIRTY-ONE TOBACCO, SIX TOBACCO AND SNUFF)

High Street in Markethouse, 1781, at the corner of High Street and Cornmarket, today's Dunnes Stores
Ann Street (a total of eight in this street; the earliest 1802 – Hugh Kearns, and three dating to 1839)

GLUE MANUFACTURERS

Williamson, North Queen Street 1791
Samuel Tucker, Sandy Row 1813
Samuel Tucker, Hill Street 1824
Belfast Glue Works, Waring Street 1833

COACH MANUFACTURERS

John Galvin & Co., Gregs Entry 1794
John Wright, Princes Street 1807
William McConnell, Smithfield Farming Utensil Manufacturing 1807
Wilson & Flanagan, South Mews 1807
Thomas Christian, Marlborough Street 1807

Belfast Coach Factory, Victoria Square 1824
Smith & Wright, Fountain Street 1824
Daniel Carty, Castle Street 1839
Martin, Gloucester Street 1839

HAT MANUFACTURERS (TWELVE IN TOTAL)

John Robinson, Ann Street 1807
Joy Davis, Bridge Street 1807
Robert Wright & Co., Church Street 1824

SHOVEL MANUFACTURER

Millars Court 1813

ROPE, SAIL AND TWINE MANUFACTURING

Waring Street 1813
North Queen Street 1839
Queen's Square 1839

STRAW BONNET MANUFACTURERS (THIRTY-ONE IN TOTAL)

Margaret Orr, Arthur Square 1824
Elizabeth Finlay, Church Lane 1824
High Street (five in total) – Ann and Marianne Cochrane 1824
Ellen McBride 1824
Jane King 1824
Ursula McBride 1824
William Hynds 1824
Mrs Bennett, Academy Street 1839
Kelly, Berry Street 1839
Castle Street (three)
Ann Burnett, Trafalgar Street 1839
Jane Charles, William Street 1839
S. Moffatt, York Street 1839

GLOVE AND BREECHES MANUFACTURING

John Rodgers, Ann Street, 1824
Samuel Johnston, Castle Street 1824

SWEET MANUFACTURING

John Mullholland, Dunbar Street 1839

SOME OF BELFAST'S WHISKEY PRODUCERS

Belfast, at the height of its whiskey production in the nineteenth century, was producing up to 3,000,000 gallons each year, equal to 60 per cent of the total whiskey production in Ireland. (Note that Irish whiskey is spelt with an 'e' as opposed to the spelling of Scottish whisky.)

W.J. Jury

W.J. Jury produced two popular brands of Irish whiskey: Special Jury and Grand Jury. Jury's specialist whiskey was probably not as well known as those produced by Dunville & Co., but it earned its reputation more by word of mouth than advertising. The name whiskey is derived from the Celtic *usque-baugh*, 'water of life', and Jury's specialist whiskey was accepted by many judges as far superior to any contemporary brand.

The outlet for Jury's whiskey was at 11 Chichester Street. The Company claimed that 'Jury Whiskeys are not blends – they are specially prepared, unmixed, unmingled and carefully matured to delight the palate of those who are competent to appreciate and ready to approve first class liquor.'

The Special Jury whiskey was a pure malt whiskey characterised by the essential qualifications of good age and unquestionable integrity. It was sold in two classes, one being 13 years old, the other not less than 20 years old. The quality of these two whiskeys and the many other brands that came out of Belfast helped to maintain the worldwide fame of the Irish distilleries.

W.J. Jury was also the proprietor of the Imperial Hotel at the corner of Castle Lane and Donegall Place; a four storey building designed by Sherry and Hughes and opened in 1868. It was a well-known hotel throughout the world and was a favourite haunt of commercial travellers. The building survived up until the 1960s when it was demolished.

Dunville & Co.

John Dumvill, as he was then known, joined the company of Napier & Co. in Bank Lane in 1801. They were whiskey blenders and tea importers. By 1807, with his name now changed to Dunville, he became a partner in Napier and Dunville. By 1825 the firm was called Dunville & Co. and it was then that it moved to Callendar Street. In 1837 Dunville & Co. launched their best-known brand of whiskey, VR, to celebrate the ascension to the throne of Queen Victoria. Dunville married Ann Douglas and they lived at Richmond Lodge on the Holywood Road.

John Dunville died in 1851 and the thriving business of Dunville & Co. was carried on by his son, William Dunville, who with his partners built the Royal Irish Distilleries. Their advertisements carried the proud boast of being 'awarded 25 prize medals'. Their head office was in Arthur Street. The distillery, on the Grosvenor Road, had lofts with a capacity to hold 6,000 tonnes of grain. The fermenting vessels could hold 35,000 gallons of liquid. The buildings on this site covered 7 acres, and they had a work force of 450 men. They had bonded warehouses in Adelaide Street, Alfred Street and Franklin Street and an impressive London office on Shaftesbury Avenue. The Adelaide and Alfred Street bonded warehouses were a short distance from St Malachy's Catholic Church. The company approached the parish priest of the church to request him to soften the ring of the church bells as the vibrations from the noise were affecting the whiskey in the bonded store.

The last Dunville family connection with the company was Robert, who died in 1931 at the age of 38 while on a trip to South Africa. He had only been chairman for 19 months. His private collection of animals was donated to Belfast Zoo at Bellevue, which opened to the public in 1934.

The Dunville Company went into liquidation in 1936. John Dunville is buried in an impressive grave in Clifton Street Graveyard. The name Dunville is mostly remembered today through Distillery Football Club, now known as Lisburn Distillery and originally on the Grosvenor Road, formed in 1880. Dunville Park is on the Falls Road. In 1890 the company was able to boast an output of 2,500,000 gallons of whiskey. Today, sadly, there is very little whiskey production in Belfast.

THE COTTON AND LINEN TRADE IN BELFAST

The Cotton Trade

Whereas Belfast began as an outlet for linen, yarn and cloth produced outside of the town, cotton manufacture had its beginnings in the town. The poor house, opened in 1774 by the Belfast Charitable Society, introduced cotton spinning in 1777. As the young people were to be employed in the poor house in 'Productive Labour'. In 1779 the poor house was advertising 'the sale of cotton thread, yarns of various degrees of fineness, cotton candlewick, gloves and stockings'. The advertisement also highlighted the fact that the products were made by the younger inmates of the house. The production of cotton yarn spread to the many small kitchen houses of the poor to be found in Belfast in the late eighteenth century. Mills were also established throughout the town, including a cotton mill in Waring Street owned by Mr John Haslett. Other mills sprang up around Millfield, Smithfield and North Street.

The earliest of the larger cotton mills was built in Frances Street in the Smithfield area. By 1790, 500 cotton looms were in operation in Belfast, and this would increase to 600 looms by 1806. The town's cotton mills reached their pinnacle of cotton production in 1826. It was the fierce competition from the Lancashire cotton mills and Andrew Mulholland replacing his York Street cotton mill, burnt out in 1828, with a flax-spinning mill that saw the demise of cotton manufacture in the town as many other cotton mills followed the example. In 1836 a parliamentary commission reported that the manufacture of cotton in Belfast had almost ceased. Today, Belfast is principally remembered for the mass production of linen with cotton seldom getting a mention.

The Linen Trade

The manufacture of linen on any scale around the outskirts of Belfast can be traced back to the influence of Huguenots (French Protestant refugees) such as Louis Cromellin. In 1699 the linen trade was reported to be of little consequence. There was no expertise in managing and working the flax, spinning, bleaching the cloth or working with the looms. At this time flax spinning and weaving were carried out by hand, a home industry that contributed to household income, as farmers often paid their rent with yarn they sold in the local market for cash.

Towards the end of the eighteenth century many bleach greens were to be found on the outskirts of Belfast. The town also built up a reputation for improvements in spinning, hand weaving and bleaching. In 1764 Dr James Ferguson discovered the benefit of adding lime to the bleaching process. He was awarded a prize of £300 from the Linen Board in Dublin for this discovery.

The bulk of linen cloth and yarn produced in Ulster was sold through the Linen Hall in Dublin. The advantage of building a Linen Hall in Belfast was that it was closer to the source of the linen cloth and yarn and, just as important, was cheaper to access.

From the 1700s to the 1840s there were up to fifty-nine cotton, linen and muslin manufacturers in Belfast:

Rosemary Street 1781 (cotton), in the abandoned sugarhouse building, operated by Thomas McCabe (the famous anti-slaver) and Henry Joy (cousin of the famous patriot Henry Joy McCracken)
Willson, F. Joy & Co., Falls Road 1786 (Cotton)
Millfield (Cotton) 1796
James Joy & Co., Winecellar Entry (Cotton) 1800, nowadays associated with Whites Tavern, a 1780 building that claims its history back to the early 1600s.
Townsend Street Spinning Mill (Cotton) 1805
Union Street (Muslin and Cotton) 1805
Clonard Mills 1806
Shankill Cotton and Spinning Manufactory
Robert Finlay, Castle Street (Cotton) 1807

Linen Manufacturers
Blackstaff Flax Spinning Mill, Durham Street 1830
Linfield Flax Spinning Mill, Rowland Way 1833
Connswater Spinning Mill 1834
Robert Gamble, Falls Road Spinning Mill 1835
Robert Thompson, Flax Spinning Mill, Donegall Street 1839
York Street Flax Spinning Mill, built on the site of a former cotton mill that was burnt down in 1828 and rebuilt as a flax spinning mill in 1832

Muslin Manufacturers
John Bell & Co., Kent Street 1807
John White, Millfield 1807
George Snell & Co, Peters Hill 1807
Margaret McCracken, (Sister of Henry Joy McCracken) Rosemary Street 1807

John White, Smithfield Square 1807
Neil McQuillan, Queen Street 1808
William Manning, Chapel Lane 1824
Thomas O'Neill, Exchange Place 1824
James Calvert, Lancaster Street 1824
Henry Magill, Library Street 1824
Robert Workman & Co, Little Patrick Street 1835
Morris & Co., Talbot Street 1835
Robert Dalglish & Co., Curtis Street 1839

BELFAST: SHIPBUILDERS TO THE WORLD

The name and reputation of Harland and Wolff in the history of shipbuilding in Belfast tends to overshadow the contribution made by earlier pioneers.

A number of 50-ton wooden ships were built in Belfast by Presbyterian ministers in the seventeenth century. One particular ship called *Eagle's Wing* was built to take Presbyterian citizens to the brave new world of America. Unfortunately, after being caught up in a storm, it had to return to port and never completed the journey.

The next serious attempt at shipbuilding was by the Ritchie Brothers. William Ritchie was building ships on the Ayrshire coast from 1775, and by 1790 three shipyards had been established on this coastline. Some of Ritchie's customers were from Belfast. In 1791, with a slowdown in orders at his Ayrshire yard, William Ritchie took up an invitation from some Belfast merchants to discuss setting up a shipbuilding industry in Belfast. The Ballast Board, responsible for Belfast Harbour, built a 'graving platform' (used for repairing ships) as an incentive to bring William Ritchie to Belfast.

On 3 July 1791, Ritchie came to Belfast, bringing with him ten experienced workmen and shipbuilding equipment that enabled him to begin the serious business of building ships in the town. His brother Hugh joined him at his yard in the Old Lime Kiln Dock close to Corporation Street on the County Antrim side of the river and on 7 July 1792 they launched their first ship, the *Hibernian*, followed by two others for a company called the Newtraders.

William and Hugh Ritchie completed a new graving dock, Clarendon Dock No. 1, in November 1800, and this was capable of accommodating two 300-ton ships. William's brother, Hugh, left to form his own shipbuilding company just north of the graving dock. When Hugh Ritchie died in January 1807 another of Ritchie's brothers, John, came over from his yard in Ayrshire to take his place. In 1811 John invited Alexander McLaine to join him and the firm was known from then on as Ritchie & McLaine. Meanwhile, William Ritchie continued to build ships and in 1810 launched the *James*, which was 100 tons heavier than the 400-ton *Hibernian.*

By 1812 William had built thirty-two ships and his brother John had built eight. He also employed forty-four journeymen carpenters, fifty-five apprentices, as well as blacksmiths, joiners and sawyers. In 1820 the firm of (John) Ritchie & McLaine built a steam vessel for George Langtry (whose grandson married Lily Langtry – Jersey Lil), a Belfast ship owner, and appropriately Langtry named his ship the *Belfast*. This ship weighed 200 tons and was 115 feet in length. Its two 70-horsepower engines were supplied by Coates and Young's Lagan Foundry.

When William Ritchie retired from his shipyard business in 1820 he handed over the management to another Scot, Charles Connell, and the name was changed to Charles Connell & Sons. Due to the continued success of both companies, in 1826 the Ballast Board completed a second graving dock. John Ritchie died on 4 April 1828 and his partner, Alexander McLaine, took over the business and renamed it Alexander McLaine & Sons. There were now two shipbuilding concerns, Charles Connell & Sons and Alexander McLaine & Sons, producing ships on the County Antrim side of the Lough.

When William Ritchie died in 1834, aged 78 years, a local journalist, Frank Finlay wrote that he should be remembered as the man who started regular shipbuilding in Belfast. There is a fine portrait of William Ritchie, by Thomas Robinson, in the Ulster Museum. All three Ritchie brothers are buried in the upper section of Clifton Street Graveyard.

Harland and Wolff

Edward Harland was born in Scarborough on 15 May 1831. He was educated at the Edinburgh Academy and left in 1846 to serve his engineering apprenticeship at Robert Stephenson & Co. in Newcastle upon Tyne. During his time at Newcastle he met Gustav Schwabe, a man who would play an important role in his future business in Belfast. Schwabe came from a wealthy Hamburg family and was a partner in the Liverpool shipping firm of John Bibby and Sons. It was through this connection that Harland got a job in Glasgow at J. & J. Thomson Marine Engineers, a company that was involved in building ships for the Bibby line.

In 1854 Robert Hickson & Co. opened a shipyard on Queen's Island, Belfast. Edward Harland, aged 23, moved from Newcastle to Belfast as manager of Hickson's shipyard. In 1857 Harland brought over Gustav Wolff, a nephew of Gustav Schwabe, to Belfast to work as his personal assistant. Robert Hickson had opened the shipyard as an outlet for material from his iron foundry in Eliza Street. He was not a shipbuilder and because of financial pressures he sold the business to Harland on 1 November 1858. A purchase price of £5,000 had been agreed. To help complete the deal, Harland received assistance from his uncle's friend Gustav Schwabe. The new name for the firm was Edward James Harland and Company.

The connection to Bibby Shipping Company of Liverpool, through Gustav Schwabe, lead to orders for three ships of 270 feet in length and 34 feet in beam. They were the *Venetian*, the *Sicilian* and the *Syrian*. These first three ships were based on Harland's radical flat-bottom design and became known as Bibby's Coffins. His critics in Liverpool referred to Harland's ships as Belfast Bottoms. They predicted that the Bibby ships might leave the Mersey but would never return. A further order for six ships soon put an end to this scurrilous criticism of what was a very successful design. In a few years Wolff's design was being copied by other yards.

Gustav Wolff, who was originally employed as Harland's personal assistant, was asked to join the company as a full partner. In 1861 the famous name of Harland and Wolff appeared for the first time. They received orders from the White Star Line, owned by Bruce Ismay, a man whose name would be controversially associated with the maiden voyage and sinking of the White Star Line *Titanic* in 1912.

Harland and Wolff also had dealings in the 1860s with the Confederate States in the American Civil War. The Union General-in-Chief of the United States Army, Winfield Scott, came up with what became known as the Anaconda Plan. Part of the plan was that the Union Navy would blockade Confederate ports to prevent cotton exports to Europe. Harland's contribution was the supply of fast steamers to the Confederate Navy to evade the blockade.

In 1871 a ship called the *Oceanic* was launched from the Harland and Wolff slipway. This was the first order from the White Star Line. Many further orders were to follow.

In 1874 William James Pirrie, who was working as an apprentice in the yard, joined the board of Harland and Wolff. He later became chairman of the company.

The last ship to be launched in Belfast at the end of the nineteenth century was the second *Oceanic* liner, the largest ship of its time. It was 704 feet long, and with a gross tonnage of 17,274 it surpassed the SS *Great Eastern*, a ship designed by Isambard Kingdom Brunel that was launched in 1858. The SS *Great Eastern* was 692 feet long and could carry 4,000 passengers. Although the second *Oceanic* liner was launched in 1899, after the death of Sir Edward Harland, it had been designed several years earlier under his personal supervision.

In 1885 Harland was elected Mayor of Belfast Town (it did not receive the status of a city until 1888), an office he held for two years. In the same year he was knighted, a reflection of his public and private services to the town. He was also an active member of the first Non-subscribing Presbyterian Church in Rosemary Street. In 1889 he was elected MP for north Belfast. In December 1895, after a long and successful career in both public and private life, he died and was buried in the City Cemetery on the Falls Road. Many hundreds of shipyard workers walked with the funeral cortege to the cemetery. A statue was erected to him in the grounds of City Hall. It stands just to the left of the front of the building, and just behind this is the memorial to the victims of the *Titanic.*

It was during the ownership of Harland and Wolff by William Pirri (later Viscount Pirri) that the *Olympic* and *Titanic* were built. As Pirri retained the original name, many people think Edward Harland was involved in this enterprise even though he died in London in 1895. Harland and Wolff built many famous ships over the years: the 1895 *Oceanic*, the *Olympic*, *Titanic*, *Britannic*, HMS *Belfast*, *Seaquest*, which was a triangular oil rig that sceptics claimed could not be built, and the *Canberra*, but most people remember it for the ill-fated *Titanic.*

The Launch of the Titanic

It was in May 1911 that the launch took place of the RMS *Titanic.* This was the sister ship of the *Olympic*, previously launched in 1910. Both ships were acknowledged as the two largest vessels afloat and were almost identical in design. Thousands of guests and spectators, including Lord and Lady Pirrie, converged on the Harland and Wolff shipyard. Lord Pirrie, as chairman of the shipyard, had been involved with Alexander Carlisle and Thomas Andrews Junior in the design of the *Olympic* and *Titanic.* The White Star Line, which had commissioned three ships (the third was the *Britannic*), had a stand for their guests, who included the American millionaire businessman Pierpont Morgan.

One of three other stands was reserved for the press, with over one hundred expected. The Lord Mayor of Belfast Mr McMordie and his wife were among the many invited guests on the launch day. The Harbour Commissioners provided space at Albert Quay for spectators and the charge for admission was donated to the Children's Hospital in Queen Street (this building later became a police station) and the Ulster Hospital for Children and Women. Even though the space allocated in the Albert Quay was extensive it was already full an hour before the launch. The General Manager of the yard, Mr Nance, arranged that all the trams coming to Queen's Road would travel fully loaded to allow for the vast crowds expected. Approaching noon, Lord Pirrie left the stand to carry out a last inspection before the official launch began. The *Titanic* then weighed approximately 26,000 tons as it was yet to be fitted out with its engines, funnels and all the internal fittings, which would bring its final weight up to around 46,000 tons.

The ceremony was due to begin at 12.15 p.m. At 12.05 p.m. a red flag was hoisted on the stern of the ship, which was followed by the firing of three rockets, and at exactly 12.13 p.m. the *Titanic* made its first motion towards the river Lagan. It only took 62 seconds to reach the water, and with the aid of heavy chains and anchors the *Titanic* came to rest in less than half its length (which was 882 feet, or 270 metres). The thousands of spectators and guests applauded the spectacle and for almost three minutes. Once the *Titanic* had settled safely in the river the tugs, with their sirens blasting, took the ship to the deep water wharf to receive its giant engines. The White Star Line had chartered the *Duke of Argyll* steamer to transport the members of the English and American press to Belfast from Fleetwood. The telegraph department of the Belfast Post Office was kept busy, transmitting about 300,000 words from the various members of the press reporting back to their news-rooms.

Mr Samuel J. Payne, speaking at a lunch held for the press, included in his congratulatory speech, according to the *Belfast News Letter* (1 June 1911), something he may have regretted later: 'He did not see anything which need cause them alarm regarding the prospects for the future.' Concluding his speech, 'He felt sure that the hope of all of them was that at no distant date they may have something at least equal, if not superior to the vessel they had seen launched that day ...'

In less than a year the same press would have a different story to report when, on 15 April 1912 at 2.20 a.m., the *Titanic* sank. She was on her maiden voyage to New York and it was ironic that her sister ship, the *Olympic*, making its return journey from New York to Liverpool, passed the scene where the *Titanic* sank. The *Olympic* was the ship that after the launch of the *Titanic* took Lord Pirrie, Bruce Ismay of the White Star Line, Mr Pierpont Morgan and other guests back to Liverpool.

Bruce Ismay sailed on the maiden voyage of the *Titanic* and, controversially, was saved while approximately 1,500 passengers and crew perished. At the Board of Trade Inquiry, Ismay was accused of interfering with the design of the *Titanic* in that he had reduced the number of lifeboats on board and had ignored warnings given to him by the *Titanic*'s Captain (Edward Smith) that the ship was travelling too fast in an area with icebergs. (The *Titanic* was fitted with fifteen watertight bulkheads, which had led some commentators to claim that it was unsinkable, but five of the sections were penetrated by the iceberg, which was sufficient to sink the ship in only three hours.) Bruce Ismay was also called to give evidence to a Senate hearing in Washington, at which he consistently denied any responsibility for the sinking of the *Titanic*.

4

CHURCHES, EDUCATION AND CHARITY

FRIAR'S BUSH GRAVEYARD

There is an old map dating back to 1570 that shows a mass of forests surrounding Belfast and beside them two buildings that are identified: Belfast Castle, on what is today's Stanmillis Road, and a friary shown on the map as Friarstown. There is a claim that the history of Friarstown goes all the way back to the fifth century, and there is even a stone purporting to come from that period, although it may have been placed there in the early twentieth-century by Francis Joseph Biggar, a Belfast solicitor and renowned historian. The Friar's Bush area was in use as a graveyard from 1601 and was used by Catholics for the saying of mass during the era of the 1690s Penal Laws.

In 1817, 1832–33 and in the period of the Great Irish Famine, 1845–51, up to 1,200 bodies were buried in the north side of the graveyard. The deaths were due to typhus, cholera and dysentery. In 1869 it ceased to be the main burial ground for the Catholic population of Belfast, a function that was taken over by Milltown Cemetery on the Falls Road. The Belfast City Council took over the running of Friar's Bush in 2000 as it was no longer in use; guided tours are available through the Belfast Welcome Centre and it is certainly worth a visit.

BELFAST'S MOTHER CHURCH

The mother church of Belfast was to be found in the area of what is today's Shankill Road and was known as the White Church and was recorded in a papal bull of 1306 (Ecclesia Alba). It was in ruins by 1604 and the parish church was transferred to the Little Church of the Ford (Capella de Vado) in High Street, which was also recorded in the papal bull of 1306, and which dated back to the tenth century. It was rebuilt as the Anglican Corporation Church in 1622, so called because members of the town corporation had to attend services there. The Corporation Church was taken over by Belfast Presbyterians in 1644 and they in turn were turned out in 1649 by Colonel Venables on behalf of Oliver Cromwell's parliamentary army. When the Corporation Church was handed back, in around 1657, to the Anglican congregation, it was in a poor state and in need of repair: Colonel Venables had turned the church into a citadel, had housed his horses inside it and had used lead from the roof to make musket bullets.

THE OLD CORPORATION CHURCH

Sited in High Street, the old Corporation Church was demolished in the 1770s when St Anne's Church was opened in Donegall Street and the former church grounds were used for burials. It was not until 1816 when John Bowden, an architect from Dublin, designed the present-day St George's Church.

ST ANNE'S CHURCH

St Anne's Church in Donegall Street lasted until the 1890s. In 1894 the new vicar, Henry O'Hara, decided to replace it with a cathedral more befitting Belfast as a city, as Belfast had become in 1888.

The first architect to work on the new St Anne's Cathedral was Sir Thomas Drew and the foundation stone was laid by Leitia, the Countess of Shaftesbury, on 6 September 1899. It was built in stages and finally completed in 2007 when the controversial metal spire was added to this Hiberno-Romanesque building.

To appreciate its history properly requires a visit. The only person to be buried in St Anne's Cathedral is Sir Edward Carson, the Dublin lawyer and leading anti-Home-Ruler.

ROSEMARY STREET AND ITS THREE PRESBYTERIAN CHURCHES

Although only one church still exists in Rosemary Street, back in the 1720s there were three Presbyterian churches in this small street. It sums up the strength of Presbyterianism in Belfast that the only other church was the Church of Ireland Corporation Church in High Street (site of the present-day St George's).

When Sir Arthur Chichester was granted Belfast as part of his reward for the defeat of Gaelic Ulster, his plan in 1608, when he was Lord Deputy of Ireland, was to colonise Ulster with Protestant 'planters'. Into Belfast he brought over a mixture of Anglicans from his home county of Devon and lowland Scottish Presbyterians. By the 1640s, after the attempted Irish rebellion, Presbyterians in Belfast began to outnumber Anglicans. Sir Arthur's revised plan was to 'Protestantise' the Catholic population as he realised there were not enough planters taking up the option of life in Ulster. In Belfast there were very few Catholics and the Presbyterians established their first Session in 1644, taking over the Anglican Church in High Street. In 1649 Cromwell's troops, who captured Belfast after a four-day siege, banned the Presbyterians from the town. They would not make an appearance again in Belfast until the restoration of the monarchy in 1660.

By the 1680s the Presbyterians had built a meeting house in Hercules Lean at the corner of what is now North Street and Royal Avenue, and by 1695 they had moved to Rosemary Street. With the increase in the Presbyterian population, a second church was built in 1708, just behind the first. Controversy arose in 1720 with a decision by the first and second churches to become non-subscribing, which meant they did not accept the man-made Westminster Confession of Faith. Members of the two churches who did subscribe built a third church a short distance down the street. So, by 1722, there were three churches in Rosemary Street; the first and second were non-subscribing churches and the third church remained subscribing.

All three churches received income from renting out pews. The renter of the pew could also charge a fee if he transferred it to another church member. As an example, Captain John McCracken, a member of the third church, on 29 September 1763 paid John Clark £11 for the transfer of pew number one. It is interesting to note that this pew was described as 'below stairs' and not up at the front of the church. It may have been Captain McCracken's choice or it may have been the only pew available at the time.

By the late 1790s there were five Presbyterian churches in Belfast, one Church of Ireland church, St Anne's Church and one Catholic church, St Mary's. In 1896 the second church on Rosmary Street closed its doors and is now in Elmwood Avenue and known as All Saints; it is still non-subscribing. The third church was destroyed in the 1941 Blitz of Belfast. A new church was opened on the North Circular Road, Belfast, but retained an association with its former home through the name of Rosemary Church. All Souls, also retained an association with Rosemary Street, naming its community hall Rosemary Hall. The first church is still fully working and remains in Rosemary Street.

BERRY STREET PRESBYTERIAN MEETING HOUSE

As you enter Berry Street from the nearby Castlecourt shopping mall, you will notice on the corner of the street a little building which houses a mid-nineteenth-century Presbyterian meeting house. This meeting house has associations with a controversial minister, Revd (Roaring) Hanna, who would later move to Carlisle Circus and St Enoch's Church. The original meeting house in Berry Street dated back to the 1770s.

ST MARY'S, CHAPEL LANE

St Mary's was the first Catholic church to be re-established in Belfast. It shows the openness of the Protestants of Belfast that they contributed almost 80 per cent of the cost of building it. On the opening day in May 1784, the Belfast Volunteer Company, who were all Protestants, led by Captain Waddell Cunningham, lined up outside St Mary's as Father O'Donnell entered to say the first mass, with the soldiers following him in for the service. It is also recorded that on the day a further £87 was collected and given to Father O'Donnell towards the building costs.

It has to be remembered that the Penal Laws, introduced in the 1690s, were still on the statute books, and so, for example, Catholic emancipation would not be introduced until 1829. Before St Mary's was opened in 1784 Catholics would meet in secret to say mass at Friar's Bush, on the outskirts of the town. A house owned by a Mr Kennedy in Castle Street was also used by the parish priest for

saying mass and a cabinet from this house acted as a makeshift altar. The plan was that if the house was raided by soldiers, the chalice and other items could be hidden away quickly in the drawers of the cabinet. It is fascinating that the mass cabinet has survived and that Father Boyle, the parish priest of St Mary's, has incorporated it into the present-day altar, where it holds the Blessed Sacrament.

Another interesting fact is that the pulpit from the old Corporation Church in High Street, demolished in the 1770s, was given to Fr O'Donnell by the vicar of Belfast, Revd Bristow, when St Mary's opened. This pulpit, dating back to the early 1600s, is now in full use in St Mary's.

ST PATRICK'S CHURCH, DONEGALL STREET

St Patrick's was the second Catholic church to be re-established in Belfast. It was opened in 1815 and was similar in style to the 1784 St Mary's Church. Again the majority of the finance to build the church came from the Protestant community of Belfast. The present cathedral-like church dates back to the 1870s. There is a famous painting by Sir John Lavery entitled *The Madonna of the Lakes* on display in the church, just to the left as you enter. Also of interest, on the right-hand side, is a stained-glass window that depicts the original, small church of 1815. Both St Mary's (1784) and St Patrick's (1815) were forbidden, under the Penal Laws, from having crosses, bells or a steeple, but sketches of the churches show them with crosses on top.

Space does not permit a list of all the churches in Belfast, which number over fifty, and the following is merely a selection of those churches that have either changed use or are now just a memory.

THE CHAPEL OF CROOK KNOCK (1615)

This was sited between the river Blackstaff and the river Lagan and was consecrated in 1615.

CHRIST CHURCH

Known as a 'Free Church', this was consecrated in 1830 and seated 1,600 and unlike almost all other churches of this period, in which pews were rented, many of the seats were free. It is sited at the corner of College Square North and Durham Street and is no longer a serving church. The Royal Belfast Academical Institution nearby took it over and it is now part of their technology suite.

FISHERWICK PLACE PRESBYTERIAN CHURCH

This was built in 1827 at a cost of £7,000 and has since been enlarged. It is now home to the Presbyterian Assembly, and has a shopping mall on the ground floor. The name Fisherwick alludes to a title given to the 1st Marquis of Donegall in 1790 when the family resided in England.

WESLEYAN MEETING HOUSE

Situated at Donegall Square East, the pillars that are all that remain of this beautiful 1806 church now front the headquarters of the Ulster Bank.

METHODIST CHAPEL, YORK STREET

Opened in 1838, this was destroyed in the 1941 Belfast Blitz.

SOCIETY OF FRIENDS MEETING HOUSE (1812)

Situated in Frederick Street, this building is now used by the charity Concern Worldwide. The Quakers have a building directly behind it.

QUAKERS MEETING HOUSE

Situated in North Street, this was opened in 1803 and was the Quakers' first meeting house in Belfast before moving to Frederick Street.

BAPTIST CHAPEL

Completed in 1819, this was situated in King Street but no longer exists.

Before concluding this section, it is pertinent to include the Jewish population of Belfast. As far back as 1652 it is recorded that a Jewish tailor named Manual Lightfoot was plying his trade in Belfast. In 1869, when the Jewish population still numbered only twenty-one, a local merchant called Daniel Joseph Jaffe, originally from Hamburg, funded the first synagogue in Great Victoria Street. As the Jewish population in Belfast increased, a larger synagogue was opened in Annesley Street, just off the Antrim Road, near Carlisle Circus.

In 1907 the Jewish community established the Jaffe Public Elementary School on the Cliftonville Road, which survived the 1941 Blitz but was destroyed later in a firebomb attack. In 1967, with a smaller Jewish community, a third synagogue was opened on the Somerton Road, and it is this that serves the Jewish community of Belfast today.

EDUCATION

The first school to be established in Belfast was a Latin school founded in 1666 by the Earl of Donegall. It was at the corner of Ann Street and Church Lane, which was then called School House Lane. By the 1840s there were over 200 places of learning. The following are just some examples:

1750: Mr Guitar's Fencing School was held in the Market House at the corner of High Street and Cornmarket.

1755: William Carmichael's English School in Shaws Entry, which no longer exists.

1760: The famous liberal educationist David Manson opened his school in High Street. This was one of many sites he used to teach Belfast's children. The other locations were Legges Lane, which no longer exists, Rosemary Street and Donegall Street.

1757: George Rupton's Writing School, Donegall Street.

1760: John Thompson's Evening Mathematical School, Broad Street (now Waring Street).

1765: Woods and MacOughtry's Boarding School, North Street.

1764: Jane Pulvercroft's Embroidery School, Pottinger's Entry.

1767: Jeremiah Crane's French School.

1771: Dumont's Dancing School, in the Market House, High Street.

1776: Poor House School, Clifton Street.

1778: Mr Pye's Flute School (unknown location).

1780: Mrs Ware's Boarding School for Young Ladies, Donegall Street.

1780s: Henry Joy McCracken and his sister Mary Ann opened a school for poor children in the Market House in High Street.

1786: The minister of the First Presbyterian Church in Rosemary Street, Revd Dr Crombie, opened an academy just off Donegall Street. Today it is called Academy Street, acknowledging the history of the school. The Revd Crombie became the school's first principal. The tradition, carried on after his death, was that the minister of the church would also be principal of the school. The school moved to Cliftonville Road in the north of the city in the late nineteenth century and has been known since then as the Belfast Royal Academy. It is the oldest surviving school in the city.

1800: A Union School was opened, to cater for up to forty poor children. Martha Matier mentions this school in one of the many letters that wrote to her brother Dr Drennan.

1802: A Belfast Sunday School was opened, so called as it only operated on Sundays, because the young men who ran the school were employed in their other jobs from Monday to Saturday.

1807: William Percy advertised in the *Belfast News Letter* that he was opening a school at 1 Pottinger's Entry, just off High Street. He was offering lessons, four times a day, beginning with his morning school (8–10 a.m.), then a day school (10 a.m.–3 p.m.), evening school (4–6 p.m.) and night school (7–9 p.m.). As part of his advertisement he highlighted that his school, called appropriately, Mr Percy's School, was 'supplied with the purest pipe water'.

1810: The first large Sunday school was opened in 1810 in Frederick Street, and employed Joseph Lancaster's method of educating young children. Lancaster, a Quaker, had devised a simple and inexpensive method of teaching a large number of children in English and maths. It was known as the Lancastrian System and the school was called the Belfast Lancastrian School, with the finance to build it coming from a lottery. Lancaster described his method of teaching as a 'mechanical system of education', requiring only one master, who would teach the eldest children, with that knowledge passed on in turn down the line until it reached the beginners. As a Quaker he did not consider restricting entry on grounds of religion, and some elements in the town, including some of the churches, objected to this form of integrated education. The school could accommodate up to 700 pupils, 500 male and 200 female, and all its running-costs were covered by donations from the public. It opened every day except Sundays.

1811: James Sheridan Knowles, a relation of the famous Brinsley Sheridan, opened a boys' school in nearby Crown Entry, off High Street. On one occasion he called on some of his advanced scholars to come into the school to write an essay. The boys had previously returned essays, written at home, which Knowles suspected were not all their own work. When he had gathered the boys in the upper room of the school he asked them to write a composition on the 'Nature of Virtue'. He then locked the boys in the room and after many visits back to check up on them he discovered that not one had completed the task. He gave up teaching, realising that his real talent was as a playwright, and in 1815 his first play, *Caius Gracchus*, was well received when it was performed at the Theatre Royal in nearby Arthur Square. He moved to Glasgow in 1817, where he also put on his play, before finally settling in London, where in 1820 he successfully staged his play *Virginias* at Covent Garden. He wrote many other successful plays including *The Hunchback*, which was performed in Covent Garden in 1832.

Belfast Academical Institution

Members of the First and Second Presbyterian Churches in Rosemary Street were the main movers behind the establishment of the Belfast Academical Institution. In 1807 Doctor William Drennan was able to report to his sister Martha that over £6,000 had already been collected towards the building costs, although this enthusiasm for the new institution was not shared by everyone. In 1807 a memorandum was issued, on behalf of the Belfast Academy, opposing the establishment of the new academy, on the grounds that there was no need for another educational institution in the town.

The Belfast Academy had been opened in 1786 by Dr Crombie, minister of the First Presbyterian Church, in a lane alongside St Anne's Church. He was its first principal and when he died in 1790 he was replaced by Revd William Bruce. The memorandum,

issued in 1807 by Revd Bruce, as Principal of the Belfast Academy, pointed out that 'This town has for some years been in possession of an excellent plan of school education ... it is indebted to the Belfast Academy founded in 1786.' The memorandum continued by highlighting that the Belfast Academy was 'The most extensive school in the counties of Down and Antrim', and then made the case against the need for another academy to be opened, although there were no objections 'To the establishment of any number of private schools that the enlargement of the town may require.' It was claimed that there was a mere 'trifling' number of teachers of the classics envisaged for the new academy, and it was argued that by spreading the teaching of the classics between two institutions, 'Belfast might be soon incapable of sending a finished scholar to Dublin College.' The attack continued: 'Application for signatures for the new academy was made only to gentlemen in business of unsuspecting liberality.' The last word, 'liberality', highlights that the main objection was that this was a plan of New Light Liberal Presbyterians, which was an allegation that would probably have been accepted to the proposers of the new academy, but they would have objected to the statement that 'as to the notion of a college it is a whimsical idea'. The memorandum continued to pour scorn on the idea of a new 'Liberal' Academy in Belfast and finished dismissively: 'this project will in the end prove abortive.'

The Belfast Academical Institution opened its doors in 1814, and the beautiful Georgian building in College Square East, designed by Sir John Soane, is still in the business of education today, known since the 1830s as the Royal Belfast Academical Institution (Inst).

National Schools

There were two national schools in Donegall Street in 1828, later run by the Christian Brothers, as well as Brown Street Day School, which began life as a Sunday school, and the Revd Dr Drummond's school at Mount Collyer, which at the time was on the outskirts of town.

Queen's College

Queen's College opened in 1849, as one of three non-denominational colleges in Ireland, the other two being located in Galway and Cork. Its purpose was to provide university education to those who could not attend Trinity College Dublin, which was allied to the Church of Ireland.

Queen's University, which achieved independent university status in 1908, has produced many famous graduates, too numerous to list, which serves to highlight that Belfast has a well-deserved reputation as a place of learning that can be traced all the way back to the opening of the Earl of Donegall's Latin School in 1666 when its population was only around 1,000.

CHARITY

The Belfast Charitable Society was founded in 1752 when rich Belfast merchants met in the George Inn and formed a committee of nineteen members. Included was the Earl of Donegall, absentee

landlord and owner of most of eighteenth-century Belfast. The origin of their charitable endeavours can be traced back to a 'Poore's Fund' which was set up in 1631 when the Sovereign Edward Holmes died and included in his will 'To the Poore decayed inhabitants of Belfast £40'.

Donations built up over the years and the names of the original donors were recorded on a charity board held in the Corporation Church in High Street. Today it can be found in the Board Room of Clifton House.

In the late 1760s the Belfast Charitable Society discussed opening a home for the poor and sick and in August 1771 the Sovereign, Stewart Banks, laid the foundation stone on a 19-acre site bordering Clifton Street and North Queen Street. The majority of the £7,000 cost of building the home was raised through a lottery. The poor house opened its doors in December 1774 with seven beds for the sick, four double beds for sturdy beggars, twenty-two double beds for the poor and four single beds for vagrants. All the physicians who attended the sick in the poor house provided their services free.

It is important to point out that this was a poor house, not the much later (1839) and notorious government-provided workhouses. The poor house also included an infirmary with a dispensary and the visiting doctors would see patients from outside the house on Tuesdays and Saturdays.

In the 1780s, cotton production was introduced into the basement of the house. The inmates also fared much better when it came to meal times, with a mixture of bread, cheese, milk, broth, rice and porridge, and on Sundays beef and veal.

The poor house, now called Clifton House, survives to this day and has been modernised internally, but the beautiful Georgian structure outside has been preserved.

Fever Hospital

The first fever hospital in Ireland was opened in 1794 in Factory Row, today's Berry Street. Again it was enabled by the efforts of the Belfast Charitable Society. The fever hospital would eventually move to a much bigger building in Frederick Street. It closed down as a hospital in the late nineteenth century.

Belfast's First Maternity Hospital

The maternity hospital was part of the original plan for the poor house in Clifton Street, as a department where poor women could give birth. The Humane Female Society applied to the Poor House

Committee but their request for a maternity ward to be included in the dispensary was turned down. On 4 January 1794 the committee rented a house at 25 Donegall Street and placed six beds on the first floor. It was referred to as a 'Lying-In Hospital', not a maternity hospital. Mrs Martha McTier, secretary of the Humane Female Society, wrote about this to her brother, Dr William Drennan, who was practising as an obstetrician in Dublin. He wrote back to her with advice on running the hospital and added: that most important thing to remember was to put above the ward 'Wash Hands Thoroughly'. He advised her that this sign should be positioned above the ward. Dr Drennan was way ahead of his time as even today this is still a major problem in modern hospitals. He never got the credit for this medical advice – that accolade went in the mid-1800s to Oliver Wendel Holmes from America and Semmelweiss of Vienna. Again all the doctors who attended the hospital provided their services for free. The Donegall Street Lying-In Hospital would move to bigger premises in Clifton Street in 1830.

There was an eligibility test for entrance into the hospital. A pregnant woman would be admitted by presenting a written recommendation of a member. A certificate was also needed from a respectable householder confirming the woman was married. Even this certificate had to be countersigned by a committee member.

In the grounds opposite the poor house, between 1794 and 1830 the hospital admitted hundreds of poor women into their building to have their babies in a safer environment, and on leaving the hospital a supply of baby clothes was given to the mother. After a further move to Townsend Street it would find its present-day home in 1904, the site of the famous Royal Victoria Hospital.

The House of Industry

Another of the projects to provide work for Belfast's adults and children was a house of industry. It was opened in, 1809 to provide work, like spinning flax for adults and preparing oakum (fibres from old ropes) for children. The work also included cotton weaving, spinning of wool and knitting.

When you compare the Belfast Charitable Society's provision of the poor house, a fever hospital and free medical attention for the poor, the house of industry, with its much stricter rules and regulations, was more in line with the later workhouses. As an example, the committee set up to run the House of Industry highlighted that the main reason for establishing it was 'to abolish mendacity (beggars) by preventing or removing its cause'. In Victorian times the attitude to begging and paupers was highlighted in a report that divided paupers into three categories: the old or those with chronic disease, who should be dealt with by the poor house; the sick, who should be dealt with by the fever hospital and dispensary; and those who could at least contribute to their own support. The third category resulted in the house of industry being set up.

The Committee who ran the house would keep coming up with ideas for, as they would put it, 'clearing the streets of ... Strolling Vagrants', who they pointed out were difficult to arrest and confine in jail. The committee even had the authority to appoint constables to apprehend vagrants. One positive innovation of the House of Industry Committee was the opening of a savings bank:

on Friday 5 January 1816 the Belfast Savings Bank was opened in the house. This bank grew from its small beginnings to become a main player in Belfast's banking system and moved from the house of industry to a purpose-built bank in nearby King Street. That building no longer exists and the savings bank was taken over by one of the larger banks, in its head office in Arthur Street, a building that is today an upmarket restaurant and bar called The Vaudeville.

Belfast's Water Supply

The Belfast Charitable Society took over the business of supplying the town's water in 1795. Between 1795 and 1840 the Society spent around £30,000 providing an infrastructure to supply Belfast's ever increasing demand for water. The business of supplying Belfast's water was eventually transferred, after an Act of Parliament, to the newly formed Spring Waters Commissioners. As part of the deal the Belfast Charitable Society received £800 and a 1-inch pipe to supply free water to the society's Poor House in Clifton Street. The £800 payment is still paid today to the society but I am not sure if they still get the free water supply through the 1-inch pipe!

5

THE CASTLES, RIVERS AND BRIDGES OF BELFAST

THE CASTLES

The first 'castle' in Belfast was no more than a motte (mound) and bailey. It was erected on the orders of John de Courcy, a Norman knight, in the 1170s as he and his soldiers made their way to Carrickfergus, where he built a more substantial castle. Belfast was a strategic crossing point from County Antrim to County Down and was referred to by the Normans as Le Ford. The name was a reference to the sandbank-crossing over the river Lagan where it entered Belfast Lough, then known as Loch Lao – The Loch of the Calves. John de Courcy's simple fort was to protect this strategic crossing. The site is now occupied by British Home Stores in Castle Lane/Castle Place.

In December 1316 Robert Bruce arrived in Ireland, passing through Belfast, to join his brother Edward. Between them they captured land as far south as Limerick until the famine caused them to return to Ulster. Robert returned to Scotland but his brother met an unhappy end when he was killed in October 1318 at Faughart, near Dundalk.

The second castle to be found in Belfast is a tower house recorded in one of the many sackings of Belfast that occurred in 1470 and 1476. In 1489, Hugh Roe O'Donnell also attacked and destroyed the castle: in the *Annals of the Four Masters* it is recorded that after O'Donnell had captured the lands of the MacQuillans, he headed to Belfast where he captured 'and destroyed the Castle of Belfast'. In 1503 and 1512 the castle was again taken and destroyed, this time by Garret Mór Fitzgerald, the Earl of Kildare.

In 1573 the Earl of Essex, sent to Ulster by Queen Elizabeth I, decided that Belfast was a more strategic place for settlement than Carrickfergus. The earl built a castle at Fort William overlooking the northern shore of Belfast Lough. Sir Brian McPhelim O'Neill, the Gaelic Lord of Clandeboye, harried Essex's troops and eventually

Essex agreed to hand over the castle to him. A feast was held in the castle to which Essex was invited. After three days of feasting, Essex arrested O'Neill, his wife and his brother and put the rest of his clan to the sword, including 'men, women, youths and maidens', as recorded in the *Annals of the Four Masters*. O'Neill, his wife and his brother were taken off to Dublin where they were executed. The Gaels of Clandeboye, on hearing of the death of O'Neill, rose in rebellion, causing Essex to return to England.

In 1611 the foundations were laid for the most impressive castle in Belfast. Sir Arthur Chichester, in a patent of 1603, was granted the Castle of Belfast, Upper and Lower Clandeboye, as well as other lands throughout Ulster. It was a reward for his contribution to the defeat of Gaelic Ulster. In 1611 he set about erecting a castle on the same site as the previous castles, to defend the strategic crossing over the river Lagan. The 1,200,000 bricks required came from an area called Sandy Row, and the castle was surrounded by a large, deep moat. This castle was in use up until a tragic fire in 1708. In 1706 the 3rd Earl of Donegall had been killed fighting in Spain and the castle, although not completely destroyed by the fire, was eventually abandoned. The Donegall family did not return to Belfast until 1802, when they built an impressive country residence just over the river Lagan on the site of today's Ormeau Park.

The present and last Belfast Castle, a Scottish baronial-style building, was built in the 1870s, on the slopes of the Cavehill, as a family home. In the 1930s it was presented to Belfast by the Earl of Shaftesbury, whose connection with the Chichester family had begun when he married Harriet Chichester in the late nineteenth century. It was his family money that helped complete the building. Today many Belfast people are only aware of the 1870s castle situated on the Cavehill and do not realise that the castles of Belfast have a history stretching all the way back to the twelfth century and a Norman knight named John de Courcy.

THE BELFAST RIVERS

The Lagan and the Farset

Most Belfast people today are probably aware of at least two local rivers: the Lagan and the Farset. The Lagan rises outside Belfast, crossing County Down and passing through Dromara and Lisburn and reaching the Sand Bank Ford, where it enters Belfast Lough. The Sand Bank Ford (the ancient crossing point) relates to the second river, the Farset, which rises in Squires Hill in the north of Belfast. On its journey to the lough it passes through many areas of the city: Ballysillan, Ardoyne, Shankill Road and Millfield, down the back of Castle Street, along Bank Street and under the front door of the Bank Buildings (Primark), down Castle Place, High Street and Queen's Square and entering the Lagan just above the present-day Queen's Bridge and Lagan Lookout. There is an archway just to the left of the Lagan Lookout where the Farset enters the Lagan.

The River Blackstaff and its Tributaries

The Blackstaff was called 'Owenvarra' (the River of the Stakes), which refers to the wooden staves that acted as a makeshift bridge across this river. On a map of Belfast, before the Blackstaff was diverted, it is shown as a wide river flowing down what is today's Chichester Street, William Street South and Victoria Square. It was the Earl of Donegall, in the 1660s, who diverted the river, and now, after passing under the Boyne Bridge (also known as Salt Water Bridge), the Europa Bus Centre, Great Victoria Street, Dublin Road and the Ormeau Road, it enters the river Lagan where it passes through the former Gas Works site.

The Ballymurphy River

This river reaches the Blackstaff at the appropriately named Bog Meadows. The fast-flowing tributaries of the Blackstaff, rising high above Belfast, were sources for use in the bleach works and bleach green industries to be found along the banks of the rivers.

The Connswater River

This river rises on the County Down side of Belfast and flows down into the river Lagan. As far back as the early 1600s a corn mill was built by the DeBeers family, who built a dam to drive their corn-grinding machinery. Up until the 1840s the firm of Owen O'Cork were milling corn there before they moved into flax spinning. Two other rivers, the Knock and the Loop, were tributaries of the Connswater. The banks of the Connswater saw the establishment of two distilleries, called Avoniel and Connswater. With the growth of the Harland and Wolff Shipyard in nearby Queen's Island, demand grew for a rope works and so the Belfast Rope Works, the biggest in the world, was opened, employing up to 4,000 people. Although the rope works is now just a memory of Belfast's industrial past, the Connswater river itself is still fondly remembered as highlighting Belfast's history.

The river was named after an Irish chieftain, Conn O'Neill, who in the sixteenth century was the largest landowner in North Down.

The nearby Castlereagh Road (Irish for 'Grey Castle') alludes to this chieftain. His castle was the stronghold of the Clandeboye O'Neills and although there is no evidence of it now, the early sixteenth-century Connswater Bridge still survives, just upstream from the Beersbridge Road.

The Derriaghy River

This river is a tributary of the river Lagan and in the 1820s its banks were the site of four bleach greens and a bleach mill that utilised the power of the river to work their machines.

The Colin River

This rises in Johnston's Green near Divis Mountain and enters the river Lagan at Dunmurry. As it runs down to the river Lagan it flows through a valley, appropriately called Colin Glen, which is now protected within National Trust property.

The Forth River/the Ballygomartin River and the Clowney River

The Forth river begins its journey down into Belfast from approximately 400 metres up on the slopes of the Divis Mountain. The Mount Gilbert Standing Stone, dating back to pre-Christian times, is to be found on the banks of this river.

The Ballygomartin river joins the Forth river and both make their way down towards the Blackstaff with the Forth river, nearing the 50 metre contour line, becoming known as the Clowney river. As was the case with the fast-flowing rivers of Belfast, bleach greens ran along the Ballygomartin river and a mixture of bleach works, brick works and flax-weaving works grew up alongside the Clowney river. At its lower reaches, the Clowney river meets the Blackstaff river at Broadway Roundabout.

BELFAST BRIDGES

As Belfast has many rivers, so it has a corresponding number of bridges.

Connswater Bridge

The oldest surviving bridge in Belfast, dating back to the early 1600s, provides a crossing point across the Connswater river.

Boyne Bridge

Boyne Bridge is the next oldest bridge and can be found where Durham Street meets Sandy Row. It was renamed the Boyne Bridge in 1937 when the 1642 bridge was built over. Its original name was the Saltwater Bridge, which was more appropriate as it was the limit of the incoming saltwater tide from the river Lagan meeting the outflowing Blackstaff river.

Shaw's Bridge

The original oak bridge built by Captain Shaw in 1655 was replaced in 1709 by the five-arch bridge that is widely in use today, as it leads to the famous Giant's Ring.

Four Bridges

Where the river Farset flows down through Belfast to the Lagan, it passes under many small bridges. For example, as it flowed through Ardoyne there were three small bridges that it passed under at Alliance Avenue, the bottom of Brompton Park and Butler Street. As it entered the town along High Street it flowed under: Chaddes Bridge which is opposite today's Cornmarket; Stone Bridge, opposite Bridge Street; Eccles Bridge, named after Sir Hugh Eccles and opposite Pottinger's Entry; and Sluice Bridge, opposite Skipper Street. All these bridges were built over in the 1770s and the river Farset, which still flows down to the sea, is now buried beneath High Street and Queen's Square.

Old Long Bridge

This bridge began life in 1682 and was completed in 1688. It was built across the river Lagan at the ancient crossing point where people would cross over from the County Antrim side to the County Down side of the river when the tide was out. The bridge was put to the test in 1689 when the Duke of Schomberg's troops arrived in Belfast from Bangor. Thousands of troops and, more importantly, the heavy artillery caused the structure to weaken. In 1692 seven arches collapsed and until it was repaired the only way across the river Lagan was by Shaw's Bridge, a few miles upriver. Not long after being repaired it was damaged again when a ship was blown against it in a storm. New restrictions were then introduced on ships berthing near the bridge. All ships had to be well moored, with a penalty of 40 shillings (£2) for anyone not complying.

The Long Bridge was the constant object of visitor approval. In 1788 a report on the bridge in *The Compleat Irish Traveller* states 'It is one of the most stately in the Kingdom'. The article goes on to mention the cost of building the bridge and quotes two figures, one of £8,000 and a second of £12,000; in the same article Belfast Lough is still referred to as Carrickfergus Bay. The bridge was an important link between Belfast town in County Antrim and Ballymacarrat in County Down. The dividing line between the two counties, Antrim and Down, was estimated to be the third arch on the County Antrim side of the river. In 1819 the safety of the Long Bridge was again questioned and a surveyor, Mr Larkin, highlighted some concerns and suggested the erection of a new bridge. It was in 1841–42 that the Old Long Bridge was demolished and replaced with Queen's Bridge, which, with some alterations, is still in use today.

The Chapel of the Ford

Built in the eleventh century, on the site of the present-day St George's Church (Church of Ireland) in High Street, this was where travellers would give thanks for safely traversing the river at low tide. The old Long Bridge is long gone but fortunately today there is still the magnificent Andrew Nicholl painting of the 1688 bridge to contemplate and enjoy.

The river Lagan passes through many bridges in Belfast on its way down to the sea: the King's Bridge (in the Stranmillis area), the Ormeau Bridge (under the Ormeau Road), the Albert Bridge (also known as the Halfpenny Bridge, when you had to pay a toll to cross it), the Queen's Bridge, the Queen Elizabeth Bridge and, more recently, two new bridges including the Dargan Railway Bridge, named after the nineteenth-century engineer Dargan who was responsible for widening the channel to allow larger vessels access to the heart of the town.

There is a photograph taken in 1901 of people at low tide on the river Lagan paying an old one penny to cross the river on a simple rowing boat, when not far to their left is the Albert Bridge which would have provided a much safer and comfortable crossing. It is an echo of ancient times before there were any bridges and people crossed the Lagan only when the tide was out to get from County Antrim to County Down.

6

ARTS, MUSIC, ENTERTAINMENT AND SPORT

THEATRE

Belfast's vibrant theatrical scene is served by the Lyric, the Grand Opera House, the brand new MAC Theatre, Brian Friel Theatre at Queen's and the Black Box. It has its own theatrical identity, reflective of the division and sectarianism that have marked its existence. Two of the most influential plays in Belfast's theatrical history are *Mixed Marriage* (1911) by St John Ervine, which examines the consequences of a proposed marriage between a Protestant and a Catholic, and Sam Thompson's *Over the Bridge* (1960), which looked at sectarianism in the shipyards. The later established the legitimacy of drama about working-class Belfast life and in September 2013, a new bridge was named after Sam Thompson. Graham Reid's trilogy, *The Billy Plays* continued within this tradition as did the plays of the late Stewart Parker. The city is well serviced by a tremendous array of writing talent. Whilst each playwright brings their own individualism to the craft, all are products of their environment, mixing black humour and social observation with a keen eye for local language and attitude. This allows serious issues to be examined in an often humorous context.

(Sarah) Marie Jones (b. 1951)

Jones started in theatre as an actress before turning her hand to writing. *Stones in his Pockets* (1999) won the Laurence Olivier Award for Best New Comedy in 2001. To date Jones has written nine plays including *A Night in November* (1994) and *Women on the Verge of HRT* (1995).

Martin Lynch

His best-known stage plays include: *The Interrogation of Ambrose Fogarty*, *Rinty*, *Holding Hands at Paschendale*, *Chronicles of Long Kesh* and (with Grimes and McKee) *The History of the Troubles (accordin' to my Da)*. He has also directed and written numerous plays for BBC radio.

Gary Mitchell (b. 1965)

Mitchell started his career at BBC Radio 4 before working with the Tinderbox Theatre Company. From a working-class background, the question of identity looms large in works such as *In a Little World of Our Own* (1997), whilst renewal and second chances are addressed in *Re-energize* (2013) with original music from John and Damian O'Neill of the Undertones. Whilst firmly rooted in a Belfast experience, his plays have been performed in London, Australia and New York.

LITERATURE

Belfast has strong links with many of the greats of English Literature. Charles Dickens made three visits to Belfast in 1858, 1867, and 1869, the last two featuring appearances at the Ulster Hall for readings. He described Belfast as 'a fine place with a rough people'. Anthony Trollope worked for the General Post Office in the Customs House in Belfast for several years in the late 1840s, a fact that is marked by a blue plaque. He wrote *The Warden*, while working there. Edgar Allen Poe's grandfather was a minister at First Presbyterian Church on Rosemary Street.

There are numerous other authors, poets and writers with strong Belfast associations including Bernard McLaverty, Brian Friel, John Hewitt, Louis MacNeice, Seamus Heaney, Michael Longley, Ian McDonald, Tom Paulin, Medbh McGuckian, Paul Muldoon, Leontia Flynn, Stephen Connolly, Alan Gillis, Lionel Shriver, Lucy Caldwell, Stuart Neville, Sam Miller and John Hewitt. Samuel Beckett taught briefly at Campbell College and when reminded that he was teaching the 'cream of Ulster' is reputed to have replied, 'Yes, rich and thick!'

Jonathan Swift (1667–1745)

From 1764–65 Swift was a minister at Kilroot, just outside Carrickfergus. There's a theory that the giant in *Gulliver's Travels* came from the silhouette of the Cavehill, observed by Swift as he travelled into Belfast to court Jayne Waring, whom he referred to as

'Varina'. *The Belfast Rental Books 1850, The Encumbered Estates* indicates an area on the present-day York Road near the old Midland Hotel called Lilliput Farm. 'Varina', whose family owned a tannery in Waring Street, Belfast, lost interest in Swift, hastening his return to England before he later moved to Dublin, where he became the Dean of St Patrick's Cathedral and wrote *Gulliver's Travels*.

C.S. Lewis (1898–1963)

Born in east Belfast, C.S. Lewis and his brother Warren were sent to boarding school in England after his mother's death in 1908, returning regularly to Belfast for holidays. He became an atheist at 15 and converted back to Christianity in 1931, becoming a member of the Church of England. His conversion and his faith are major themes in his work. Lewis was interested in presenting a reasonable case for Christianity, perhaps because of his experience of sectarian conflict in his native Belfast. He served in the First World War and lectured as a fellow and tutor in Magdalen College, Oxford. A prolific writer, his published works range from poetry to science fiction and children's fantasy novels. *The Lion, the Witch and the Wardrobe* was published in 1949, to popular acclaim. In total there would be seven of the now famous Narnia books. Lewis married an American, Joy Davidman Gresham, in 1953, but she tragically

died of cancer in 1960. His relationship with Joy Gresham was made into a very successful film, *Shadowlands*. In 1998 a statue of Lewis by Ross Wilson was erected at Holywood Arches Library in east Belfast. It portrays the author opening the wardrobe door to Narnia.

Seamus Heaney (1939–2013)
Born and raised in Co Derry, Heaney attended and later taught at Queen's University. In 2005 he was awarded the Nobel Prize for Literature. His first collection of works was the acclaimed 'Death of a Naturalist' whilst 'District and Circle' (2006) won the T. S. Elliot prize.

Brian Moore (1921–99)
Born in Belfast, Moore emigrated to Canada and later the USA. His most famous novel, *The Lonely Passion of Judith Hearn*, was made into a feature film with Maggie Smith in the titular role. He co-wrote the screenplay for Alfred Hitchcock's *Torn Curtain*.

Glen Patterson (b. 1961)
To date Patterson has written 10 novels and a memoir, the most recent of which is 'Where Are We Now' (2020). He co wrote the screenplay and stage version of 'Good Vibrations' and was BAFTA nominated.

Robert McLiam Wilson (b. 1964)
Wilson's novel *Ripley Bogle* stands alongside the great works in Irish Literature. Wilson has also published two other novels, *Manfred's Pain* and *Eureka Street*. He moved to Paris where he now resides and after a period of inactivity contributes regular columns to *Libération*. He is also rumoured to be working on a new novel.

Anna Burns (b.1962)
From Ardoyne in North Belfast, her third novel *Milkman* won the 2018 Booker Price. Set during the Troubles in the 1970s, it concerns an 18 year old girl's encounters with an older man who is a paramilitary. Belfast is not named but is clearly referenced. In 2021, she was elected a fellow of the Royal Society of Literature.

FILM

The first major film to be set in Belfast was Carol Reed's film noir *Odd Man Out* (1947). The film does not specifically mention Belfast but the majority of outdoor scenes were filmed in the city and notable landmarks such as Queen's Bridge and the Albert Clock are featured. The final scenes are set in the Crown Bar which was re-created as a studio set at D&P Studios in Denham, Buckinghamshire. James Mason played the part of Johnny McQueen who is injured after a failed IRA robbery and hides out whilst trying to get to a ship to take him to safety. The film won the BAFTA award for best film in 1948 and in later life Mason cited it as his favourite as did filmmaker Roman Polanski.

Kenneth Branagh's critically acclaimed, *Belfast* (2021) is a coming of age story set at the outset of the Troubles. Whilst the film is set in Belfast, it's central themes are emigration and the reasons behind it. Rich in metaphor, filmed in black and white, it was nominated for several Academy Awards and Golden Globes and won the Oscar for best screenplay. In 2023, "An Irish Goodbye" won the award for best short film at the Oscars. Shot entirely on location in Northern Ireland, the black comedy follows the story of two estranged brothers coming to terms with the death of their mother.

In 1997 the government-funded Northern Ireland Film and Television Commission (now called Northern Ireland Screen) was established. Its aim is to promote the development of a sustainable film, animation and television production industry. The old Harland & Wolf Paint Hall is now a film studio and a growing industry has emerged that encompasses local and international productions. Perhaps the most successful being *Game of Thrones*.

The director Brian Desmond Hurst (1895–1986) was from east Belfast and is perhaps best known for *Scrooge* (1951), starring Alastair Sims. Lisa Barros D'Sa and Glenn Leyburn are directors whose *Cherrybomb* (2009) starring Rupert Grint of Harry Potter fame and *Good Vibrations* (1013) have both been critically acclaimed.

Terry George (b. 1952)

George is from Belfast but moved to the USA in the early 1980s. He debuted as a playwright in 1985 with *The Tunnel*, a play about the 1976 prison escape attempt from Long Kesh. The play was the first of numerous collaborations with writer/director Jim Sheridan. In 1992 George and Sheridan wrote *In the Name of the Father*. The film was nominated for seven Academy Awards including Best Screenplay. In 1996 George was named Young European Film Director of the Year for his directorial debut Some Mother's Son.

Since then he has written and directed numerous television shows and feature films including, *A Bright Shining Lie*, *The District*, *Hart's War*, and *Reservation Road*. In 2004 he wrote, directed and produced *Hotel Rwanda*. The film was nominated for four Academy Awards, including Best Screenplay. In 2016 he wrote and directed 'The Promise' staring Oscar Isaac, Charlotte Le Bon and Christian Bale. Imprisoned during the Troubles, George moved to the USA in the early 1980s and eventually secured a visa. He wrote and directed the short film *The Shore* which his daughter Oorlagh produced and which won an Oscar in 2012.

Since the 1980s, Belfast has featured in a lot of Troubles-related films most notably, *Hidden Agenda* (1984), *In the Name of the Father* (1993), *Nothing Personal* (1995), *Some Mother's Son* (1996) *The Boxer* (1997) *Resurrection Man* (1998) *Titanic Town* (1998), *Mickybo and Me* (2004), *Fifty Dead Men Walking* (2008), *Hunger* (2008) and *Shadow Dancer* (2012). Recently films with story lines outside the Troubles have emerged, most notably *Man About Dog* (2004), *Cherrybomb* (2009), and *Cup Cake* (2010).

Good Vibrations (2013) is a biopic of record label owner Terri Hooley. *Like the Boxer* (1997) concerns reaction against the endemic sectarianism of 1970s Belfast. Central to this is punk rock music at a time when rebellion in Belfast was to stand against the old certainties of prejudice. As the main character announces to an ecstatic crowd, 'New York has the haircuts, London has the trousers but Belfast has the reason!' It's a realistic but ultimately positive portrayal of Hooley a man as flawed and as wonderful as his native city.

ACTORS

Belfast has helped produce some fine dramatic talent. Siobhan McKenna won a Tony Award for her 1955 Broadway debut in *The Chalk Garden* and was featured on the cover of *Life* magazine. She also appeared in *Doctor Zhivago* and *The Landlady* directed by Roald Dahl, as well as *King of Kings*, playing the Virgin Mary. Actor Joseph Tomelty starred in *Over the Bridge* and films including *Odd Man Out*. He was also a playwright and novelist, his most notable play being *All Souls' Night* (1948). His daughters, Roma and Francis, are also actors. Sam Kydd, Derek Thompson (Charlie from *Casualty*), James Ellis (Sgt Lynch from *Z Cars*), Ciáran Hinds and Stuart Townsend are all from Belfast. Other local actors include James Nesbitt from Coleraine, Adrian Dunbar from Enniskillen, brother and sister John and Susan Lynch from Armagh and the late Ray McAnally from Donegal.

Eileen Perry (1900–73)

A silent screen actress, Eileen Perry was born in South Belfast and emigrated, aged 9, with her family to New York in 1909. At an early age she was taken under the wing of Douglas Fairbanks and moved to Los Angeles, signing with 20th Century Fox. Between 1917 and 1933 she appeared in sixty-eight films and in one starred alongside the famous Rudolph Valentino. She died in 1973 and is buried in her adopted home city of Los Angeles at the Chapel of the Pines Cemetery.

Errol Flynn (1909–59)

Flynn went to school in Belfast, attending one term at Royal Belfast Academical Institution (Inst) in 1921 whilst his father taught at Queen's University. The family later returned when his father was made Professor of Zoology at Queen's University, a fact Flynn managed to include in dialogue in the film *Dawn Patrol*: 'My father, who is Professor of Biology at Queen's University, Belfast, says man is the most savage animal on earth.' They lived at four different addresses: 4 Shrewsbury Park, 22 Harberton Park, 4 Broomhill Park and finally, up to his retirement, 40 Cadogan Park. Errol Flynn visited his family on at least three occasions and is supposed to have scrawled some uncomplimentary words about one of his female co-stars on one of the bedroom walls, possibly 4 Shrewsbury Park.

Stephen Boyd (1931–77)

Stephen Boyd's real name was William Millar and he was born on the outskirts of Belfast at Glengormley. He began acting in Belfast in the Group Theatre before moving to London. He played a spy in the 1956 film *The Man Who Never Was* and in 1957 he appeared in *The Night Heaven Fell*, opposite Brigitte Bardot which brought him to the attention of Hollywood. The role for which he is mostly remembered is as Messala in the epic film *Ben-Hur*, and for that he received a Golden Globe, although many film critics felt he should have received a Best Supporting Actor Oscar.

He was the original choice to play Mark Antony opposite Elizabeth Taylor in Cleopatra but ended up starring in *The Fall of the Roman Empire* alongside another icon of film, Sophia Loren. Stephen Boyd has thirty films to his credit and in a book about his life, *Stephen Boyd: From Belfast to Hollywood* by Joe Cushan, a letter from a film producer who had worked with him, Euan Lloyd, recalled him as being 'One of the nicest, kindest people I have met in my lifetime, rare in this profession'. Stephen Boyd died of a heart attack on 2 June 1977 in Northridge, California. His wife Elizabeth had only married him ten months earlier.

Stephen Rea (b. 1946)

Academy Award nominee as best actor for *The Crying Game*, Stephen Rea attended Belfast High School (which used to be sited at Glenravel Street). He won a place at Queen's University Belfast, leaving with a BA, and at Queen's he studied alongside the late playwright Stewart Parker. While in Dublin in the late 1970s he acted alongside Gabriel Byrne and Colm Meaney. He has worked with the Irish film-maker Neil Jordan and set up the Field Day Theatre Company in 1980 with the late Seamus Heaney, Brian Friel and Tom Paulin. He has a close friendship with the American actor Sam Shepard and has been involved in many of his plays. He was awarded Honorary Degrees by both Belfast Universities (Queen's University and University of Ulster) in recognition of his contribution to theatre and films.

Liam Neeson (b. 1952)

Although born in Ballymena in County Antrim, it was while working in Belfast that Liam Neeson would 'tread the boards' in the local Lyric Theatre. He was also featured in some early BBC Northern Ireland documentary films and many felt he should have won an Oscar for his portrait of Schindler in *Schindler's List*.

Kenneth Branagh (b. 1960)

Born and brought up in Belfast, Branagh attended many plays and was particularly inspired by Joseph Tomelty. When he was 10 his family moved to Reading, where his father had found work. He was accepted into RADA (Royal Academy of Dramatic Arts) at 18. Ironically, his break came back in his home town, when he starred in Graham Reid's trilogy of *Billy Plays* about a troubled working-class Belfast family. It proved a big hit when shown on primetime BBC television. By 1987 Branagh formed his own theatre company, Renaissance, and he played the lead in their first production, *Henry V*. A best actor and director award followed and he was nominated for, but did not win, an Oscar.

A renowned talent, he has appeared in numerous films including *Harry Potter and the Chamber of Secrets*. The theatre remains his real passion and love, highlighted by his appearances in productions of Shakespeare and Chekov. In 1990, Queen's University Belfast awarded Branagh an Honorary Doctorate of Literature for his Services to Theatre, Film and the Ulster Youth Theatre, which he continues to support. Despite moving to England when he was 9, Branagh has said, 'I feel Irish. I don't think you can take Belfast out of the boy.' He was knighted in 2012.

Jamie Dornan (b. 1982)

Born and schooled in Belfast, perhaps his most famous role was in 'Fifty Shades of Grey' (if that can be called a film). He played the father in Branagh's 'Belfast' and has appeared in numerous television dramas.

MUSIC

The single most important event in Irish musical history was staged in Belfast, in 1792, the Belfast Harp Festival. A four-day event organised by the city's radicals, it attracted ten harpers from Ireland and one from Wales and was held at the Assembly Rooms on Donegall Street. The purpose of the festival was to document music that was dying out. Edward Bunting, aged 19, was commissioned to notate the music. After the festival, he travelled across Ireland documenting traditional harp music and published three books. Without Bunting's work, a considerable body of Irish traditional music would have been lost forever. In 1993, The Chieftains, including Derek Bell from Belfast, recorded an album in tribute to him with the Belfast Harp Orchestra. Whilst historically important, the Harp Festival and harpers were not popular with all, most notably the United Irishman Wolf Tone who is reported as saying, 'Strum, strum and be damned'.

Belfast and Ulster has a fine tradition of accomplished traditional and folk musicians and singers: Sean McGuire, the McPeake family, Altan, Clannad, Four Men and a Dog as well as contemporary artists like Cara Dillon and Gráinne Holland.

Two of best known traditional songs about Belfast are:

'I'll Tell Me Ma': a children's song associated with Belfast thanks to versions recorded by The Dubliners and Van Morrison and The Chieftains.

'My Lagan Love': a traditional melody with the lyrics by Joseph Campbell, versions have been recorded by Van Morrison, The Chieftains, The Corrs, Sinéad O'Connor and Kate Bush.

A good way to sample Irish traditional music is to attend many of the sessions held in pubs around the city. Further information on these can be obtained from Visit Belfast (visit-belfast.com).

Classical Music

The Belfast Music Society runs festivals and events throughout the year and the Ulster Orchestra performs regularly in Belfast (www.ulsterorchestra.com). Belfast has also produced some world-class classical musicians:

James Galway (b. 1939)

Known as 'The man with the golden flute', Galway is an internationally renowned as a soloist. His recording of 'Annie's Song' reached number three in 1977 and he was knighted in 2001.

Barry Douglas (b. 1960)

Classical pianist and conductor, winner of the Gold Medal 1986 International Tchaikovsky Competition and founder of Camerata Ireland, Douglas was awarded the OBE in 2002.

Popular Music

Belfast has featured in numerous popular songs, in part due to its notoriety. The word 'Belfast' is often used as a shorthand illustration of the futility of war by artists as diverse as James Taylor, Orbital, John Lennon, Elton John, Simple Minds and Bony M. The quality is similarly diverse, ranging from wonderful to appalling. 'Invisible Sun' by the Police is in the former. Sting (Gordon Sumner) worked as a teacher in Whitehead and also part-time as a barman in the Red Barn Pub, just off Rosemary Street. The building still exists and today is the home to the Red Barn Gallery.

The city has also produced numerous singers and musicians, including Ruby Murray (1935–1996) who in 1955 had seven number ones, Ronnie Carroll who twice represented the UK in the European Song Contest and, in the traditional sphere, the McPeake family. In the early 1960s, the music scene in Belfast was dominated by showbands performing covers of current hits. Showbands provided an apprenticeship for many musicians, including Eric Bell of Thin Lizzy, Van Morrison and Henry McCullough. The emergence of Rock 'n' Roll helped spark a vibrant rhythm and blues scene centered on the Maritime Hotel from which Them, featuring Van Morrison, emerged.

Van Morrison (b. 1945)
After three noteworthy singles – 'Gloria', 'Baby, Please Don't Go' and 'Here Comes the Night' – Morrison's left Them and embarked on a solo career. His first solo hit single was 'Brown Eyed Girl' in 1967 and he has since delivered a stream of classic albums such as *Astral Weeks*, *Moondance*, *St Dominic's Preview* and *Avalon Sunset*. Belfast plays an important role in many of his songs most, notably on 'Cyprus Avenue' from *Astral Weeks*. To Morrison, the streets and associations of Belfast are signifiers of better times. Whatever the song, be it contemplative, celebratory or infused with Celtic soul, Belfast memories are constant themes. It's interesting that he has never written a sad song about his native city and in that his work reflects a side of Belfast that often goes unnoticed – the joy, soul and humour that's as much a part of the native psyche as the turmoil and strife for which it's better known. Morrison reflects this and it's fitting that in 2013, he was granted the 'Freedom of Belfast'.

Gary Moore (1952–2011)
Moore gained worldwide fame as a guitarist, initially with Thin Lizzy but later as a solo artist. He worked with many of the leading lights of popular music before his untimely death from heart failure at the age of 52.

The 1970s were grim days for life and music in Belfast. The city was off limits for most bands, with the honourable exceptions of Horslips and the late Rory Gallagher whose Ulster Hall shows became legendary. The city centre became a ghost town after 5 p.m. as people stayed in to avoid the bombs and murder gangs. In 1977, a wonderful thing happened to Belfast: punk rock music arrived. The two most notable bands from the era were Stiff Little Fingers and the Undertones whose iconic, 'Teenage Kicks' was recorded off Donegall Street in Belfast. There were many other bands such as Rudi and the Outcasts playing the only punk venues available, The Harp Bar and the Pound. The real value of punk in Belfast lay in creating a world beyond the straight jacket of sectarianism and hatred; as a light in some very dark times. John T. Davies' classic documentary *Shell Shock Rock* is a wonderful record of this as is the film Good Vibrations.

The punk period was short lived and the music scene and life continued much as before, a twisted version of 'normal'. Bands continued to emerge like Energy Orchard and The Adventures but there was no scene as such and bands invariably went to London.

Energy Orchard released perhaps the best song ever written about the city, Joby Fox's 'Belfast'. The Adventures were signed to a major label but despite some wonderful songs, including 'Broken Land', they never attained commercial success. Therapy? from Larne emerged in 1989 and were successful as were Ash from Downpatrick and D:Ream featuring Peter Cunnah from Derry but there was no focus or coherence, music often being seen as a way out from Belfast or Northern Ireland.

The emergence of dance culture in the early 1990s affected Belfast in much the same way as punk rock: it brought people together. There were numerous club nights in the city and DJs such as David Holmes and Agnelli & Nelson enjoyed international success. Holmes has gone on to develop a career in film soundtracks including, *Out of Sight*, *Oceans 11*, *12*, and *13*, *Hunger* and *Good Vibrations* and is an in demand producer and remixer.

Musically, Belfast is still looking forward. It has an important legacy and fine songwriters with Belfast connections, Bap Kennedy, Joby Fox, Duke Special and Foy Vance to name a few, but there is a new generation of outstanding talent emerging; Arborist (aka Mark McCambridge), Gareth Dunlop, Joshua Burnside and Acoustic Dan Gregory amongst plenty of others. Central to this is the Oh Yeah centre on Hill Street in the Cathedral Quarter which was part funded by Gary Lightbody of platinum-selling Snow Patrol. The Oh Yeah centre has a wonderful, free exhibition on local music. The days when Belfast was a ghost town at night are long gone and it has a host of venues dedicated to original music.

It is a vibrant and rich musical city ranging from trad to jazz to indie and all shades in between. There is new and exciting talent to be discovered and the best way of keeping informed is with Dig With It magazine (digwithit.com).

VISUAL ARTS

The most striking visual art in Belfast are the murals. Historically these were signifiers of territory and a means of promoting messages denied in mainstream media. The peace process witnessed a change of tone with murals depicting paramilitary organisations being replaced by those with reference to sporting or social history. Political realities in Belfast can be gauged by the nature of murals being painted and in 2012 and 2013 murals celebrating paramilitaries began to reappear. Conversely, Danny Devenny and Mark Ervine, two muralists from opposite sides of the political divide, work together on projects that reflect a common humanity. One of their recent murals is at Berry Street Presbyterian Church in the city centre and includes a depiction of nearby St Mary's Catholic Church.

The most famous classical artist from Belfast is portrait painter Sir John Lavery (1856-1941). His 'Madonna of the Lakes' is in St Patrick's Church whilst his portrait of the Earl of Shaftesbury is on display in Belfast City Hall. There is a vibrant contemporary art scene and there are numerous art galleries dotted throughout the city. Photography is well served, particularly by Frankie Quinn's Red Barn Gallery on Rosemary Street. Photographer Michael Donald's work first gained prominence in newspapers but he has moved towards portraits, his most recent work featuring the Rolling Stones. His portrait of Charlie Watts was exhibited in the National Portrait Gallery, London.

A plethora of modern sculptures have appeared in the past ten years; 'The Big Fish' by John Kindness, 'Statue of Harmony' by Andy Scott and Anto Brennan's 'Spanish Civil War Memorial' are well worth catching. A good way of partaking in the city's art life is to attend 'Late Night Art', held on the first Thursday of each month. There is a wonderful website, creativechangeni.com, documenting contemporary art following the careers of emerging artists such as Breandan Clarke, Zoe Murdoch, Christoff Gillen, Colm Clarke and Brendan Jameson. In 2021 Array Collective, a group of Belfast based artists received the Turner Prize for the installation 'The Druthaib's Ball' an imagining of an illicit pub that invites audiences to share an alternative history within its confines.

COMEDIANS

The humour in Belfast is fast, quick and dark with a large absurdest streak. In Belfast if people like you, they insult you and it's not uncommon for someone to worry when friends or acquaintances are too polite to them. Running a walking tour, I remind customers not to be alarmed should they hear people hurling insults at me; it's because I'm popular. There could be no other explanation. Verbal exchanges can best be compared to a boxing encounter, with jab and counter jab following rapidly in succession known as craic; the fun to be gained from everyday exchanges. It's engaged in wholeheartedly but always with an understanding that tongues are firmly in cheeks. It's no surprise that the city has produced some noted comedians.

James Young (1918–74)

Young was never afraid to show his audiences the stupidity of their own prejudice but did so with a twinkle in his eye and a genuine affection for the people he portrayed. His weekly TV show finished each week with the phrase, 'For God's sake stop fighting' and although he never achieved prominence outside Ireland, there's a truth to his work that still resonates today.

Frank Carson (1926–2012)

A skilled comedian, Carson's catchphrases were, 'It's a cracker!' and 'It's the way I tell 'em', acknowledging that the delivery was often better than the joke, a skill he underplayed.

Patrick Kielty (b. 1971)

Kielty first came to attention with weekly appearances at a local comedy night while studying at Queen's University. At present, there is a lively comedy scene in Belfast well served by comedians such as Jake O'Kane, Tim McGarry, Colin Murphy and Nuala McKeever.

Belfast has also nurtured a host of television personalities and commentators including Roy Walker, Gloria Hunniford, Eamon Holmes, Colin Murray, Peter Curran, Henry McDonald, Jeremy Paxman, Bill Neely, Andrea Catherwood and John 'Jackie' Wright (1905–1989) perhaps best known for being the bald-headed sidekick on *The Benny Hill Show*.

SPORT

Belfast and Northern Ireland has produced many world-class sports personalities including world snooker champion Alex Higgins, Formula 1 drivers John Watson and Eddie Irvine, champion jockey Tony McCoy and two-times Commonwealth gold medallist Mike Bull. Northern Ireland currently has three world-class golfers: Rory McILroy, Darren Clarke and Graeme McDowell. The major team sports played in Belfast are football, rugby and Gaelic (hurling or football). Belfast has produced many outstanding football players, the greatest being George Best.

George Best (1946–2005)

Best was voted European Footballer of the Year in 1968 and was named by Pelé as one of the greatest ever footballers. His skill was matched by his bravery and he became one of the world's first celebrity footballers. He was famously quoted as saying, 'I spent a lot of money on booze, birds and fast cars – the rest I just squandered'. The lifestyle led to problems with alcohol and eventually killed him. For all his problems, he was much loved in his native city and 100,000 people lined his funeral route for what was in effect a state funeral. In 2006, the City Airport was renamed after him.

The Northern Ireland international football team play at Windsor Park. Local football is semi-professional with four Belfast teams playing in the top division: Cliftonvillle, Crusaders, Glentoran and Linfield. Games are competitive as are admission prices.

Rugby

In rugby, Ulster compete professionally in the European and Celtic Leagues and were European Champions in 1999. Games are played at Ravenhill in east Belfast. Rugby is played and administered on an all island basis with a club league comprising four divisions. The Belfast teams competing in this are Belfast Harlequins, Malone, Queen's University and Instonians. A number of world-class rugby players emanate from Belfast, including Mike Gibson, David Humphreys, Stephen Ferris and Dr Jack Kyle who, in 2002, was named the Greatest Ever Irish Rugby Player by the Irish Rugby Football Union.

Gaelic

There are three main codes in GAA: football, hurling and camogie. There are club and county competitions and Antrim play at

Casemount Park in west Belfast. Antrim's men have appeared in national finals for but have never won in either code whilst the camogie team have won six all Ireland champion titles.

Boxing

As well as producing a number of outstanding fighters, boxing in Belfast has helped to develop and build relationships between people from opposite sides of the religious divide. Boxers have always moved freely between gyms and the sport has helped many young fighters avoid sectarianism and hatred. In boxing what matters is the boxing, not politics or religion.

Belfast's boxers include: Paddy Barnes (twice Olympic bronze medallist, European gold medallist), John Caldwell (Olympic bronze medallist, British Champion), Michael Conlan (Olympic bronze medallist), Darren Corbett (Commonwealth & IBO), Carl Frampton (European silver medallist), Freddie Gilroy (Olympic bronze medallist, British, Commonwealth and European), Damaen Kelly (WBC and European), Brian Magee (IBA, WBO), Eamon Magee (Commonwealth), Dave 'Boy' McCauley (IBF), Jim McCourt (Olympic Bronze Medallist), Wayne McCullough (Olympic silver medal, WBC World), Rinty Monaghan (British, European, Commonwealth and World), Hugh Russell (Olympic bronze medallist, British Champion at Bantamweight and Flyweight), Neil Sinclair (British), Sam Storey (British), Tommy Waite (Commonwealth), and many more.

Barry McGuigan (b. 1961)

Although borne in Clones, Barry McGuigan is synonymous with Belfast and attracted enormous crowds to his fights at the Ulster and Kings Halls in the 1980s. British, European and World Flyweight champion perhaps his greatest victory was in bringing people from all sides together at the height of the troubles; In 2010, McGuigan was awarded the United Nations Inspiration Award for Peace.

Athletics

Mary Peters (b. 1939)

Born in England, Mary Peters moved to Northern Ireland in the early 1950s and attended school in Belfast. While teaching domestic science at Graymount Girls Secondary School she met her future coach 'Buster' McShane. She joined his Health Studio full time in Music Hall Lane (just off Arthur Street), finishing fifth in the European Championships in 1961 and fourth in the 1964 Tokyo

Olympics. She won gold in the pentathlon at the 1972 Munich Olympics. She returned to a hero's reception in Belfast and set about fundraising for a modern athletics track which now carries her name. She retired from full-time athletics in 1974 after winning gold in the Commonwealth Games in New Zealand. In 2000, she was made a Dame which followed her MBE (1972), and CBE (1990). In 2013 she was awarded the Freedom of the City – a fitting tribute to her ongoing love of her adopted city of Belfast.

7

BELFAST'S ARCHITECTURAL HERITAGE

With Belfast only developing as a small borough in the early 1600s there is almost no real architecture of any note from this early period, except of course for the famous Belfast Castle, dating back to 1612, in the centre of town, which deserves a mention.

When King William III arrived with his troops in Belfast in June 1690, he stayed in Sir Arthur Chichester's castle and the king commented on how it reminded him of his palace in Whitehall, London. Unfortunately, this grand building was almost completely destroyed in a fire in 1708 and was never rebuilt.

As far back as the late eighteenth century, Belfast could have become a town of grand architecture, similar to cities such as Bristol or Liverpool. In 1786 there was a failed attempt to set up a Belfast Slaveship Company, which, if it had have been allowed to go ahead, would have led to Belfast becoming one of the grand cities of the late eighteenth and early nineteenth centuries, like Bristol and Liverpool, two cities that made fortunes from the slave trade.

The building in which the Slaveship Company was to be set up was the Exchange and Assembly Building, in Waring Street, dating back to 1769 with additions made in 1776, and which was at the centre of the commercial, social and political life of Belfast. In 1845 it was greatly altered by the architect Charles Lanyon when it became a bank, and has been lying empty since the bank closed in 2000. There are plans to convert this historic eighteenth-century building into a Literary Museum.

There are other buildings that stand out from the eighteenth century. The First Presbyterian Church in Rosemary Street was built in an elliptical shape by Roger Mullholland, in 1783, and still survives to this day. The poor house (now called Clifton House) was opened in 1774 with the majority of finance coming from a lottery. Even today this Georgian building can hold its own when compared with later nineteenth- and twentieth-century structures.

Another building of note was the 1785 White Linen Hall, a grand Georgian-style building that was replaced by Brumwell Thomas' 1906 City Hall.

In the early to mid-nineteenth century there was an explosion of civil and industrial buildings, which reflected the massive growth of Belfast as a world power in terms of its industrial output. It had the largest tobacco factory, rope works, shipyard and flax-spinning mill anywhere in the world. A name that is associated with this growth is Charles Lanyon, well known for the design of many iconic buildings throughout Belfast. In 1840 he designed the Palm House for the (Royal) Botanic Gardens in Belfast. The original design was of standard flat glass, but with the help of Richard Turner from Dublin he introduced, for the first time anywhere in the world, a curvilinear iron and glass structure. This preceded the more famous Kew Gardens in London.

In 1845 Lanyon designed the building that housed the Ulster Institute for the Deaf and Blind on the Lisburn Road. Today the site is occupied by Queen's University Medical Biology Centre. The original beautiful Tudor-style building was demolished in 1965 and it is believed that in some aspects it influenced Lanyon's design for Queen's College, which opened in 1849, although his plans for Queen's College also included an almost exact copy of the Founders Tower

in Magdalen College, Oxford. He also won the contract to design the university library, which is the second oldest building on the site.

After the National Trust, Queen's University is the most important custodian of listed buildings in the Province. The university includes 250 buildings; almost half are listed as being of special architectural merit.

Lanyon designed a court house and prison, lying directly opposite each other on the Crumlin Road, Belfast. He copied the fan-based shape of London's Pentonville Prison and included a tunnel between the two buildings. The court house is now closed and was badly damaged by a fire in 2009 but the jail has been refurbished and is open to visitors. Lanyon also designed the Sinclair Seaman's Presbyterian Church (1856) in Corporation Square, Belfast, close to Donegall Quay. This church contains the famous pulpit designed in the shape of a ship's prow.

There is a blue plaque on a modern building in Wellington Place, Belfast, commemorating that Lanyon once lived there, but it is the iconic buildings of Belfast that many people will remember Sir Charles Lanyon for, and many buildings have incorporated his name, for example the 1849 Queen's University Lanyon Building, the Lanyon Building just off York Road and Lanyon Place, alongside the river Lagan, which houses the Waterfront Concert Hall. One last memento that he would probably have appreciated is the Sir Charles Lanyon Memorial Prize, given to a final-year architecture student at Queen's University, Belfast. On the first floor of the Lanyon

Building at Queen's University, just above the entrance hall, are two portraits – one of Sir Charles Lanyon and the other of his wife, Lady Helen Lanyon.

Although Belfast missed out on the wealth promised by the aborted 1786 slaveship scheme, it make up for this as it took advantage of the nineteenth-century Industrial Revolution, which it embraced with vigour. In 1814 the Belfast Academical Institution was opened. This magnificent Georgian building, designed by Sir John Soane (architect of the Bank of England), sits just off College Square East and is still in the business of education. One of its former pupils was the film star Errol Flynn.

The following is a selection of outstanding nineteenth-century buildings that surround the present-day City Hall.

DONEGALL SQUARE NORTH

The Venetian Gothic building of the former Richardson Sons & Owden's Warehouse (today Marks and Spencers) by Lanyon, Lynn and Lanyon, stands proudly at the corner of Donegall Square North and Callendar Street. The building in red sandstone includes rampant lions, which were the Richardson trademark. This building is described in great detail by Marcus Patton in his book *Central Belfast* and certainly stands out as a building of great character.

THE FORMER ROBINSON & CLEAVER ROYAL IRISH LINEN WAREHOUSE

The former Royal Irish Linen Warehouse is situated at the corner of Donegall Square North and Donegall Place and was completed in 1886 to designs by Young and Mackenzie. The building is of scrabo sandstone but with red Scottish granite on the ground-floor shop fronts. Along the top of the first-floor windows is a collection of fifty busts of this famous linen store's customers, which included Queen Victoria, the then Prince and Princess of Wales and the Maharajah of Cooch Behar, to name but a few. As early as 1887, just one year after opening, one-third of all parcels leaving Belfast came from Robinson & Cleaver Royal Irish Linen Warehouse. The famous white Sicilian marble staircase with statues of Erin and Britannia at its base dominated the ground floor. Sadly, in 1987, when the building was converted into individual shops and offices, the staircase was purchased and is now in Lord Ballyedmond's castle. The original clock on top of this iconic building still acts as an accurate timepiece for the citizens of Belfast. On the ground floor, in 2013, a café was opened with access for customers to the first-floor balcony.

DONEGALL SQUARE EAST

At the corner of Chichester Street and Donegall Square East is the late nineteenth-century Pearl Assurance House (originally Ocean Buildings). It was designed by Young and Mackenzie for the Ocean Accident Guarantee Corporation. It is five storeys high, of red sandstone, and one of the many carvings on the building is the Ocean Company's trademark: mermaids holding lighthouses on shields. There are many other carved features of animals, birds, kings and queens.

DONEGALL SQUARE WEST

The Scottish Provident Institution (constructed 1897–1902) is a powerful Baroque-style building in sandstone that almost dominates this side of the square. Its Corinthian columns on plinths have individual carvings referencing Belfast's great industries: shipbuilding, rope works and linen, and there are many more features to enjoy if you can manage to draw your attention away from the ground-floor shopfronts that run the whole length of the building.

DONEGALL SQUARE SOUTH

Number 10, Yorkshire House, was built for the Jaffe Brothers, and there is a plaque to one of the brothers on the side of the building. It was originally a three-storey stone linen warehouse but today is a hotel, appropriately called Number Ten. Around the walls of the building are sixteen heads of a historic nature including Newton, Watt, Columbus, Washington, Shakespeare and Homer.

THE CITY HALL (1896–1906)

The magnificent City Hall, opened in 1906, relied on the vast profits of the Belfast Corporation Gas Department for its completion as it contributed £294,000 to the building costs of around £360,000. This Baroque-style revival building is of the best Portland stone on the outside with Greek and Italian marble used extensively on the interior. The central dome and the two corner cupolas resemble Wren's St Paul's Cathedral in London, causing some commentators to refer to it as 'Wrenaissance' architecture. The triangular pediment just below the dome features Hibernia bearing the

Torch of Knowledge and includes many other figures; by the renowned London sculptor Frederick Pomeroy, this is acclaimed as the best piece of sculpture in Belfast. The City Hall dominates Donegall Square and was a statement that Belfast was now a city (it was granted city status in 1888) and that, having grown from a population of only around 20,000 in 1801 to around 349,000 in 1901 it had arrived on the world stage.

BELFAST CASTLE (1868–70, BY LANYON, LYNN AND LANYON)

There were castles in the centre of Belfast from 1170 to 1708. The castle in 1708 was almost completely destroyed and its owners, the Donegall family, moved to England to become absentee landlords. In the 1870s Belfast Castle was built on the slopes of the Cavehill with a panoramic view over the city. It was built in a Scottish Baronial style, originally for the 3rd Marquis of Donegall, but with most of the money coming from the future 9th Earl of Shaftesbury, who had married Letitia, the 3rd Marquis' sister.

In finishing, here are three more sketches of iconic buildings of Belfast: the Boat, the Titanic Museum and the Unite Union building.

8

THIS, THAT AND THE OTHER

A MISCELLANY OF INTERESTING FACTS, HUMOUR AND MALAPROPISMS

A quotation from the famous Belfast scientist Lord Kelvin in 1883: 'X-rays will prove to be a hoax.'

Maxim Litvinov, a Russian Jewish emigré who taught in the Jaffa School on the Cliftonville Road in Belfast, returned to Russia in 1917 to fight in the Revolution and went on to become Stalin's Foreign Minister.

Chaim Herzog, who held the post of President of Israel for two terms, was born in Cliftonpark Avenue in Belfast.

Wolfe Tone, the famous Irish patriot, was visiting Belfast during the 1792 Harp Festival and recorded in his diary: 'Strum, strum and be hanged.' He also wrote: 'No new music discovered, believe all the good Irish airs are already written.'

Lily Langtry ('Jersey Lil') was married to George Langtry, the grandson of a Belfast ship owner, and old estate maps show that she owned property at one time in Fortwilliam Park just off the Antrim Road in North Belfast.

The Belfast Canal: in the eighteenth century there was a plan to run a canal from present-day Wellington Place to the river Lagan. It never got past the drawing board.

The original, 1925 plan for the parliament building was an exact copy of the State Building in Washington and was designed by Sir Arnold

Thornley. The plans had to be scaled back due to lack of finance. The original name of the nineteenth-century castle that stands in the grounds of the present-day Stormont estate was Storm Mount.

In 1787 four men, all with the Christian name John, opened up a bank that became known as the 'Bank of the Four Johns'. It was the second bank to be established in Belfast.

The first mention of linen yarn in Ireland was recorded during the reign of Richard II (1377–99).

Strange Laws: in medieval times there were some strange proceedings in court cases, for example, Petty Larceny – a prisoner could invoke his entitlement to a law called 'The Benefit of Clergy' which would result in a lighter sentence. It was originally only applied to actual clergy but was extended to anyone who could read.

When Belfast was taken by parliamentary forces after a four-day siege in 1649, a plan was formed to transport Presbyterians and some Anglicans who supported King Charles I to other parts of Ireland. The list included Lord Montgomery Clandeboye. The plan was never acted on.

Colonel Venables, who was responsible for the capture of Royalist Belfast in 1649, had also fought in the Parliamentary Army in 1643–46. In 1654 he commanded land forces sent to capture Jamaica but failed, along with Admiral Penn, and both ended up in the Tower of London.

One of the last acts of the Dublin Parliament before the 1800 Act of Union was to prevent further burials in the graveyard in High Street, Belfast. It had originally been the site of the Anglican Corporation Church, demolished in the 1770s.

With the old Corporation Church having been demolished, Revd Bristow donated the pulpit to Father O'Hanlon on the opening of St Mary's Church in 1784.

Women could attend Queen's University in the 1880s, long before they could attend Oxford or Cambridge Universities.

A street entertainer in Belfast of the nineteenth century was given the name Cocky Bendy because of the unusual shape of his legs.

One of the many old taverns that still survive in twenty-first century Belfast, Whites Tavern, has an erroneous claim that the famous patriot Henry Joy McCracken, who had been found guilty of treason in the nearby Exchange and Assembly Building in Waring Street and was taken under guard to be hanged in High Street, stopped off there to have his last drink before he met his fate!

The Crown Public House, the famous Victorian public house in Great Victoria Street, was built to cater for the opening of the Belfast–Lisburn railway link in 1839.

There is a headstone in the Clifton Street Graveyard to a well-loved and respected lecturer, Professor John Young, from the Royal Belfast Academical Institution. The headstone simply reads: 'Young! Moulders Here, 1829'.

The oldest tavern in Belfast, McHugh's, dates back to 1711.

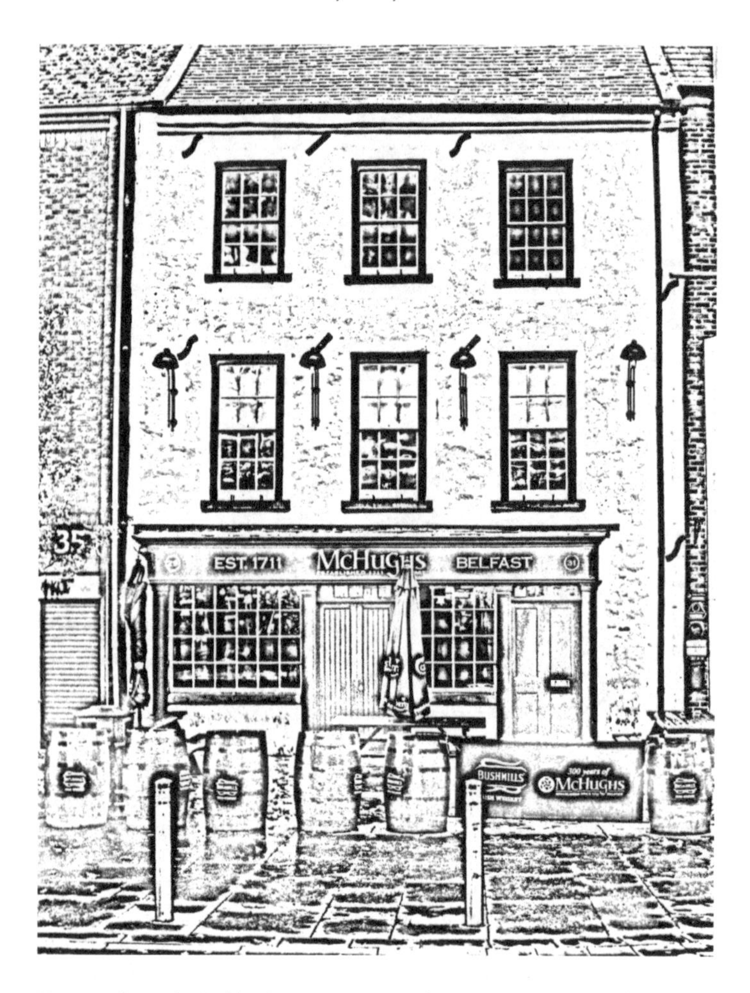

Extracts from the *Belfast News Letter* (Friday morning, 3 December 1847) during the period of the Great Irish Famine (1845–51):

> Frederick Street Fever Hospital: On the previous Saturday an athletic, delirious, fever patient, in the climax of the disease, managed to climb up the walls and attempt to throw himself from the third storey of the building (about 40 feet above ground level) out of the window on to the street below. He was weakened by the disease so could not manage to haul his body over the window sill. He hung suspended, in a state of near nudity, until he was exhausted and fell back into the arms of

> one of the nurses, a level-headed woman, who held him until her cries attracted assistance.
>
> It is now a thing of daily occurrence (in Belfast) to see haggard, sallow and emancipated beings stricken down by fever or debilitated from actual want, stretched prostate upon the footways of our streets and bridges, utterly helpless and unable to proceed from the spot where they have fallen down.
>
> In a field on the Old Lodge Road (Belfast) lay a wretched mother and her fevered boy, with his burning head on a pillow of straw, his limbs quivering under a thin blanket, his mother hopeless and helpless, shielding him from the scorching sun or whispering words of comfort ... It was not until late evening that the mother was able to get assistance to remove her child to a Fever Hospital.
>
> A poor woman with an emaciated, sickly-looking girl of about ten years old sat under the window of a shop on the south side of High Street. Attention was drawn by the heart rending moans of her mother. Passers-by saw that the little girl lay nestling in her mother's lap and she was in 'the agonies of death'. Five minutes later the child was stretched in the open fields, a lifeless corpse. Her name was Sarah George and her death was due to 'hardship and privation'. Her mother said she had had a fine boy who had died in similar circumstances three weeks earlier.

All three Richie Brothers, from Scotland, who developed shipbuilding in Belfast in the late eighteenth and early nineteenth centuries, are all buried in Clifton Street Graveyard. There is also a Ritchie Street just off York Road to commemorate their contribution to the birth of shipbuilding in Belfast.

Belfast Zoo opened in the 1930s and owed its origins to animals left from the estate of a member of the famous Dunville whiskey family.

In Clifton Street Graveyard there is a grave to the memory of Robert Hyndman which included a statue of his dog on the top. Unfortunately vandals managed to knock it off its plinth and all we have now is a photograph taken by A.C. Merrick.

Clifton Street Graveyard also contains a grave to a nineteenth-century family called Ash. On each corner an ash tree was planted. Today only one of the ash trees has survived the ravages of time.

In Joe Baker's *Snapshots of Belfast* there is an infamous photograph, taken in the 1930s, of 'Members of the Italian Fascist Party (Belfast Branch)' at the Belfast Cenotaph giving the fascist salute.

On the Custom House wall in Queen's Square is a plaque to Anthony Trollope, author of *The Barchester Chronicles*. While in Belfast as a Post Office surveyor he wrote most of his famous novel *The Warden*.

A Royal Proclamation made on 19 June 1690 by King William at 'Our Court at Belfast' prohibited plundering by the army.

MALAPROPISMS

- A local woman renowned for her malapropisms told her friends that she had got a job in the local theatre and could get them some 'continental' tickets for free entry. Also, in the days when MFI Stores were still in operation, she told her friends that she had bought herself a table at 'MI5'.
- In the nineteenth century when 3 million Irish people were reliant on the lumper potato for sustenance, a survey of the time highlighted that Irish labourers were half an inch taller than their English and Welsh counterparts.
- A malapropism spoken by a City Hall member asked to check out the film *Ulysses*: back in the 1960s the local council could decide if a film was suitable for the citizens of Belfast to see. The controversial film of James Joyce's book *Ulysses* was shown to the local councillors in the former Ritz Cinema and the BBC were waiting outside to get a reaction to the screening. The first councillor out was asked by the reporter what he thought of the film. Instead of his intended criticism regarding the film's pornographic nature, the councillor indignantly stated: 'That film was PHOTOGRAPHIC, definitely PHOTOGRAPHIC.'
- In the 1960s a local working-class MP, John McQuade, was renowned for his malapropisms. He discovered sections of the public were making allegations about him and he is quoted as saying: 'When I get hold of these ALLIGATORS...'

John Rea, an eccentric, late nineteenth-century solicitor whose office at 80 Donegall Street was nicknamed 'The Old Orange Lodge', was one day leading Orangeman, next day Nationalist. He described himself as 'her Orthodox Presbyterian Britannic Majestys Orange-Fenian Attorney General for Ulster'. His library had busts of Wolfe Tone, John Mitchell and Napoleon, a stack of pistols and swords, he had two dogs and two cats who shared his table and a parrot cage in every drawing room window (each window held four mounted grey parrots). His son and a 'Fenian' relative also lived there; she was called 'Orangemary Anne'.

TYPICAL IRISH OBSERVATIONS

- When the film-stars James Mason and Gregory Peck were in Ireland some years ago a woman approached them and enquired of James Mason: 'Excuse me sir but would you be James Mason in his later years?' The two film-stars fell about laughing and recounted the story many times to their friends.

- In Belfast some years back a BBC Film Unit asked a passer-by in the street: 'Excuse me sir. Have you lived here all your life?' And he replied: 'Not yet!'

Gordon Sumner, also known as Sting, was originally from Newcastle upon Tyne but worked in the Red Barn Pub, just off Rosemary Street in Belfast, when he was in the city to see his future wife Frances Tumelty. The pub is now the home of the Red Barn Gallery, which has gained a reputation over its short life of providing an outlet for local and international photographers. The Red Barn Gallery has built up massive library of photographs and old photographic slides portraying life over many years in Belfast and throughout Ireland.

There is an area in east Belfast on the shores of Belfast Lough that is known as Bunkers Hill, commemorating a famous battle at the beginning of the American War of Independence.

There is a shrine to Our Lady beside St Mary's Church in Chapel Lane. The shrine is set in a cave to resemble the shrine at Lourdes in France. When the cave is observed from a distance a definite outline of a man's face can clearly be seen.

Belfast Swings: not a musical reference to Belfast but to a time in the 1960s when the Sunday observance of no work and no play was taken to extremes. The council's interpretation of the Sunday laws even extended even to tying up the swings in the public parks. There was a joke going around at the time that even the budgies in their cages had their swings tied up.

Sir Alexander Fleming on one occasion attended Queen's University to speak to the Medical Society but managed to forget his papers when he left for the journey back to England. The train to Larne Harbour, the ship to Scotland and even the train to London were all held back until his papers were returned to him.

Until the 1960s, men were employed in Belfast by the local mill owners to visit the homes of their workers at 6 a.m. and, using a long pole, to tap their bedroom windows to alert them to get ready for work. They were called the 'knocker uppers'.

The Curious Case of Two Positives Meaning a Negative: some years back a lecture took place at Queen's University in Belfast. The theme was 'The Use of Language'. The lecturer, not aware of the localism in Belfast's use of English, stated that two positives can never mean a negative. Before he could continue a member of the audience shouted out 'Aye, right', meaning that two positives ('Aye'/'Yes' and 'Right') were used in a negative way in Belfast. An example: 'Can you lend me a fiver?' Answer: 'Aye, right' – meaning 'No'.

Edwin Lawrence Godkin (1831–1902) was a graduate of Queen's University in Belfast. He founded and edited *The Nation*, an iconic American magazine that influenced American life and thought. As you enter Queen's University there is a plaque to Godkin, just to the left-hand side of the inner doors.

SOME RESTRICTIVE SEVENTEENTH-CENTURY LAWS

- A fine of 5 shillings on a household who, without good reason, did not attend the Church of Ireland Corporation Church in High Street.
- The sale of wine, ale, etc. was prohibited during the Sunday service.

- On 29 March 1638 a by-law was passed for householders in the town to replace their wooden chimneys with brick and a fine of 40 shillings was imposed on anyone who did not obey.
- Ramparts were built around Belfast in 1641–42 and a cess (tax) was levied on 150 of the townspeople, who had to contribute £20 towards the building costs.
- In 1800 gun powder could be sold in the town but it had to be kept under lock and key, with a fine of £10 for anyone who did not obey this law.
- Six Belfast shoemakers in 1800 attempted to have their wages increased and ended up in Carrickfergus Jail. The judge stated, 'How could trade go on or improve if such actions were permitted?'
- In 1800, before the introduction of gas, an act was passed that included street lamps in the town with a penalty for breaking or extinguishing a street lamp of six months' imprisonment without bail. If anyone was caught stealing any part of a street lamp and found guilty, they could be transported for seven years or publicly whipped; it all depended on the judge trying the case as he would decide what the punishment would be.
- Any person begging in the streets of Belfast had to wear a badge which showed that they were allowed to beg. The idea of 'badging' the beggars came from Jonathan Swift.

A Sticky Problem: in the late eighteenth century, Belfast had two sugarhouses. The Old Sugar House Company offered a reward of £52 10s (50 guineas) to find the person who had reported to the authorities that a man had fallen into a pan of sugar and was boiled to death and that the sugar was afterwards sold. There is no record of anyone claiming the 50 guineas.

In 1773, absentee landlords away from their property for six months or more in each calendar year had to pay a tax of 2 shillings in every pound of rent collected.

The 1st Earl of Donegall, who set up a Latin school in Belfast in 1666, also funded a mathematical lectureship in Dublin's Trinity College which still exists to this day.

The early 1800s was the era of the infamous Burke and Hare's bodysnatching in Edinburgh. In many graveyards in Belfast precautions were taken to prevent bodies being robbed. One particular graveyard on the Upper Shankill Road saw a 'Watch House' being built. The money was provided by William Saxon and Israel Milliken, as protection for the recent burial of their relatives. The oldest grave in the Shankill Graveyard dates back to 1685 and this, along with the famous eighteenth-century Clifton Street Graveyard, is well worth a visit.

In 985 the native Irish who lived on the hills overlooking Belfast would have seen Viking ships approaching up what is now Belfast Lough. The Vikings did not stop in Belfast as they were only passing through in their search for monasteries to pillage.

Located at Shaw's Bridge, on the outskirts of Belfast, there is an archaeological gem, the Giant's Ring, which dates back to 2700 BC.

The Infamous Lord Donegall: when the Donegalls' castle was almost completely destroyed in 1708 with the loss of three of the Donegall children, it was decided that rather than rebuild the castle they would move to England and become absentee landlords. However, in 1802 the 2nd Marquis of Donegall arrived back in Belfast. The reason for his return was not any great love of the town but to avoid the many debts he had run up while living in England. Unfortunately, his propensity for running up debts which he could not afford to pay continued in Belfast and the Marquis quickly gained the title of 'Lord Donemall' for his habit of not honouring his debts.

Pro Tanto Quid Retribumus: this is the Belfast motto, meaning 'What return shall we make for so much'.

In the 1960s the iconic City Hall in Belfast came to the attention of Queen's University Rag Day students. The students invaded the city centre, collecting money for various charities. One student managed to get up to the large green dome of the City Hall, some 40 metres up, and paint the letters PTQ on it. *PTQ* was also the name of the students' magazine. The student was caught and the dome was repainted, but if you look closely at it today you will see three areas at the front that are not as green as the rest.

Harland and Wolff never claimed that the *Titanic* was unsinkable; that was implied in the publicity brief from its owners, the White Star Line and a shipping magazine.

The *Britannic*, the third ship in the Olympic Class, built by Harland and Wolff, was due to be named the *Gigantic*, but after the disaster of the sinking of the *Titanic* it was changed to *Britannic*.

In the historic First Presbyterian Church there is a plaque to the memory of Charles Hamilton, who in the 1780s was employed in the East India Company. The governor-general sent Hamilton back to England and after the five years he transcribed the *Hedaya*, a commentary on Islamic Law that was only updated by Islamic scholars in 2005.

Sir Charles Lanyon, who designed Belfast's Queen's University (opened in 1849), placed at the centre of the building a copy of the 1458 Founders Tower from Magdalen College, Oxford.

When the Belfast Technical College opened in 1907 in the grounds of Royal Belfast Academical Institution, it was almost an exact copy of the old War Office in London.

The City Hospital, on the Lisburn Road, was up until its inclusion in the 1948 National Health Service, the Belfast Workhouse. When the notorious workhouse system was introduced into Ireland in 1839, an infirmary was included in every workhouses, which is why nearly all the previous workhouses became local hospitals on the introduction of the NHS.

Clayton Moore, the actor who played the always-masked Lone Ranger in the popular 1950s–60s television series, at one time paid a visit to Belfast. During his stay in the famous 200-bedroom Grand Central Hotel (today the Castle Court Shopping Complex) he would come down to the restaurant for his meals wearing his Lone Ranger mask!

The Black Man is a statue of Revd Henry Cooke, a controversial nineteenth-century minister, which was erected opposite the front gates of the Royal Belfast Academical Institution, known as Inst. It replaced a previous statue of the tragic young Earl of Belfast, Frederick Richard Chichester, who died aged 26 of scarlet fever in Naples, Italy. His body was brought back to Belfast for burial and as a well-loved composer, poet and friend of Inst it was appropriate that a statue to his memory be erected in front of the school. Although in bronze, it was painted black and was always known as 'The Black Man'. In 1876 it was decided by the local council to replace the earl's statue with that of the Revd Henry Cooke and the original 'Black Man' statue was removed and is now still on display at the City Hall.

The new occupant of the site, Revd Henry Cooke, is also known as 'the Black Man', even though his statue over the years has almost completely changed from black to green. It is pointed out to visitors that he has his back to Inst as they were regarded as New Light (liberal thinking) Presbyterians whereas he was Old Light (orthodox) Presbyterian. The previous 'Black Man' statue of the Earl of Belfast also had his back to Inst even though he was a friend of the college; in his case it was not a slight but merely to have the statue facing up Wellington Place and Donegal Square North.

Located in Botanic Gardens, next door to Queen's University, is a palm house that saw the very first use of curvilinear glass, well before the more famous Palm House in Kew Gardens, London.

The 1775 the *Belfast News Letter* was the first paper outside of America to publish the Declaration of Independence even before it reached King George in London. It is therefore not surprising that Belfast was known at this time as the Boston of the North.

Glen Millar, Irving Berlin, Joe Brown, are just three famous names who were in Belfast during the Second World War, as Belfast was a staging post for US troops on their way to the conflict in Europe. There is a fine obelisk just to the left of Queen Victoria's statue, at the front of the City Hall, commemorating this historic event.

Philip Larkin was a poet and librarian at Queen's University in the 1950s. Today on the old library building there is a plaque to commemorate his time at Queen's.

There is a plaque just to the right-hand side of the chancel in St George's Anglican Church in High Street commemorating Sir Henry Pottinger (baronet), who, after the end of the Opium Wars in China, arranged the lease of Hong Kong, of which he became governor-general. This lease expired in 1997 when the last governor-general, Lord Patton, handed it back to the Chinese government. At the bottom of the plaque it states that Pottinger felt he deserved a higher honour than the title of a baronet (which is the lowest honour; next are baron, viscount, earl, marquis and duke). These are some of the actual words: 'On concluding his successful treaty with China, in the year 1842. He was destined for the peerage, but lost this high distinction through the same hostile influence ... to prevent Parliament rewarding his eminent service to the state.'

Also in St George's Church in High Street, beside the chancel, there are two large, beautiful free-standing candlesticks that draw many comments from churchgoers and visitors alike. The candlesticks had been part of a four-poster bed. As you enter St George's, just to the right is the baptismal font, where there is another beautiful candlestick which was presented to the church by St Mary's Catholic Church in Chapel Lane. This was in thanks for the gift of the pulpit, from the former Corporation Church that was demolished in the 1770s, that was presented by Revd Bristow to St Mary's when it opened in 1784. The pulpit still plays an important part in the daily masses at St Mary's.

In St George's Church in High Street and just to the left of the altar is the chair used by King William III when in Belfast in 1690 before he headed off to fight King James at the Battle of the Boyne. Visitors comment on how small the chair is and do not realise that the king was only 4 feet 9 inches tall.

As a commemoration of Harland and Wolff Shipbuilders, various sail-like structures now stand proudly in Donegall Place as Belfast. These structures display all the famous names like *Titanic* and *Olympic*, but the very last one gives details of the tender that conveyed the third-class passengers at Cherbourg onto the *Olympic* and *Titanic*. Christened the *Traffic*, it was launched on 27 April 1911 (ship no. 423) for the White Star Line for use as a tender in Cherbourg, and in the First World War it served as a troop carrier, but it was sold in the 1920s to Germany and was torpedoed and sunk in 1941.

The *Nomadic*, which transferred first- and second-class passengers onto the *Olympic* and *Titanic* in Cherbourg, was brought back home to Belfast and underwent a £7,000,000 restoration, and is now anchored and open to visitors just before the main *Titanic* exhibition building.

St Matthew's Church, on the Woodvale Road, built in 1870, if observed from above is shaped like a shamrock.

The smallest house in Belfast used to be found on Great Victoria Street. It measured approximately 3 metres across and at one time housed the sexton of the Baptist Church next door.

William J. Barre, the architect who designed the famous Albert Clock, died before it was completed. He also designed the Ulster Hall in Bedford Street.

St Enoch's Presbyterian Church, which opened in 1872 at Carlisle Circus, was built for the controversial minister Revd Hugh Hanna but was lost when it was gutted in a fire in 1985.

A Norman knight, William de Burgh, Earl of Ulster, was murdered in 1333 in an area that today is called Skegoniel Avenue, just off the Shore Road, Belfast.

The first fairs and markets in Belfast were established in 1605. They ran between Bridge Street and Cornmarket.

The famous eighteenth-century actress Mrs Sarah Siddons made her first visit to Belfast in 1775.

The first mail coach service commenced between Belfast and Dublin in 1788.

Francis Joy, who founded the *Belfast News Letter and Advertiser*, died in 1790, aged 93.

The first flying of the Union Jack in Ireland in 1801 was on the Market House in High Street.

A lunatic asylum was opened in 1829 on the Grosvenor Road, a site now occupied by the famous Royal Victoria Hospital (RVH).

Ulster – possible origin of the name:
UL: referring to the dominant tribe, the Uliadh
S: stadir (Norse for 'homestead')
TER: Irish for 'land'
Ulster: 'The land/homestead of the Ulaidh'

The following is a poem setting out the correct way of showing the Red Hand of Ulster:

> The Red Hand of Ulster,
> Right verses Left:
> The Red Hand of Ulster's a paradox quite,
> To Baronets 'tis said to belong:

> If they use the left hand, they're sure to be right,
> And to use the right hand would be wrong.
> For the Province, a different custom applies,
> And just the reverse is the rule:
> If you use the right hand you'll be right, safe and wise,
> If you use the left hand, you're a fool.

This is an adaption of the old lines on 'The Rule of the Road' (J. Vinycombe). The argument goes back to the early 1600s, during the reign of King James I, when baronets' shields showed a red hand on a white shield but it was always the left hand and never the right.

In 1847 the Choctaw Indians/native Americans, who were on a 500-mile forced march from their native land to Oklahoma, sent $170 for Irish Famine relief.

9

UP AND DOWN THE CITY STREETS

In any city, town or village you could pass by its streets and roads without appreciating the origin of their history. A good example is Belfast, from the Gaelic *Beal Feirste* (the 'approach to sandbank or ford'). The following describes the many streets and entries to be found in Belfast and how each street or entry offers up a slice of the city's history.

DONEGALL PLACE

Although not one of the oldest streets in Belfast, Donegall Place which dates back to the 1780s, certainly includes a lot of Belfast's hidden history.

Its original name was Linenhall Street, as it led up to the White Linen Hall. In 1783 Arthur, the 5th Earl of Donegall, an absentee landlord who took great interest in Belfast's development, leased land that at one time was part of the castle grounds. The Earl had surveyed the land from the corner of Grand Parade (Castle Place) through Robins' Orchard (part of the castle gardens) to the proposed site for the White Linen Hall. The street was planned as a residential development and the various leases contained requirements for houses built to be twenty-seven feet high; all girders, joists, roofing and other timbers were to be of good oak or fir. The six-foot area in front of each house (the footpath) had to be paved with flagging stones and there was also a requirement to make provision for the road in front of each house to be 'well paved with stones or pebbles.' When the area around the White Linen Hall (built in 1785) was developed and called Donegall Square, Linenhall Street was renamed Donegall Place. (Note: the first use of the name Linenhall Street (which ran from Waring Street to North Queen Street) had applied to what is now Donegall Street. That street was developed in the 1750s by the 5th Earl of Donegall who employed the architect Roger Mulholland to carry out the work.

HIGH STREET

High Street runs from Castle Place to Victoria Street and was one of the original streets of Belfast, dating back to the early 1600s. The river Farset flowed underneath it and at one time up to four bridges existed over the river: Chades Bridge opposite Corn Market (this bridge is believed still to exist under the road), Stone Bridge opposite Bridge Street (used during market days in the eighteenth century), Eccles Bridge opposite Pottinger's Entry and Sluice Bridge opposite Church Lane.

Any reference to large ships sailing up High Street in the seventeenth or eighteenth centuries is incorrect. The water level where the Lagan met the Farset was only 2–3 feet deep. All large ships had to dock at Garmoyle, 3 miles down Belfast Lough, while lighter vessels would complete the journey to the bottom of High Street. The Farset river openly ran down the middle of High Street but was covered over by the 1770s and nowadays, although diverted when the West Link road system was built, still exists all the way down beneath Castle Place and High Street to the river Lagan.

Nos 1–15: (1929) Dunnes Stores, originally built for Woolworths and Burtons, whose names still appear on top of the building. The site goes back to 1639 when a market house was built. It was extended later in the 1660s to include a courthouse. It is ironic that an ancestor of Henry Joy McCracken (who was hanged at this spot), a man called George Martin, had given the land to the town. Here in 1613, Belfast, under the control of Sir Arthur Chichester, was made a borough, one

of forty created in Ireland at the time. It was entitled to send two MPs to the Dublin Parliament and to appoint a Sovereign (Mayor) and twelve burgesses. The arrangement for the two MPs would last up to the Act of Union in 1801 and the Chichester/Donegall family would lose the privilege of deciding on the twelve burgesses in the reform of local government in 1839. This location was also the site of the gallows where the famous Presbyterian United Irishman Henry Joy McCracken, along with other United Irishmen, was hanged on 17 July 1798. McCracken had been the leader of the failed United Irish attack on Antrim. Captured just outside Carrickfergus when trying to escape, he was arrested and brought back to Belfast. He was tried by Colonel Montgomery in the Exchange and Assembly Building in Waring Street and hanged at 5 p.m. on the same day.

Next to Dunnes Stores is the famous Crown Entry, where the United Irish Society was founded in the Crown Tavern in October 1791. All of the original members of the society were prominent Presbyterian merchants. The next block houses modern shops and cafés. The only interesting note is that in the early nineteenth century the Armagh, Lisburn and Lurgan coach began its journey from this spot.

Wilson's Court is here, where the United Irishmen's paper, the *Northern Star*, was published from 1792 to 1797, until it was attacked and closed down by the Monaghan Militia. The First Trust bank occupies the block from Wilson's Court to Joy's Entry. The site was previously the premises of E. & W. Pim, who were importers of tea, wine and spices. Also previously at 31 High Street was the well-known firm of H. Johnston, whose famous gold umbrella hung outside the shop. The firm eventually moved to Ann Street along with the famous gold umbrella but are no longer in business there.

Joy's Entry: there is a plaque to commemorate the fact that the Joy and McCracken families lived on each side of the entry and at one time the *News Letter* was published there. The Joy family were of Huguenot stock, French Protestants forced to leave France when the Edict of Nantes was revoked in the 1680s. The McCracken family originally came from Scotland.

The next block runs from Joy's Entry to Pottinger's Entry. The most impressive building in this block is St George's Building of 1881. It housed Belfast's first full-time picture house, opening in 1908 to a packed house of about 1,500. It lasted only until 1916, and after the loss of the cinema audience it was used as a dance hall and was also a venue for boxing matches.

Pottinger's Entry has connections to the Pottinger family, one of whom was Sovereign when King James's troops captured Belfast in 1688. The town at this time was surrounded by a protective wall and Pottinger opened the gates to let the troops in.

Church Lane was originally called School House Lane as it was the site of a Latin school opened in 1666 by the Earl of Donegall, a nephew of Sir Arthur Chichester.

The present St George's Church (Church of Ireland) only dates back to 1816 and was designed by John Bowden from Dublin. The site can, however, trace its history back to the tenth century when the Chapel of the Ford was used by travellers who had successfully crossed over the river Lagan at low tide. The chapel was also recorded in a papal bull of 1306.

This little chapel was greatly extended into the Corporation Church in the early seventeenth century, and in 1644 the first Presbyterian session in Belfast was held in the church when the Belfast Presbyterians took it over for their services. In 1649, as Belfast was a

Royalist town, Cromwell (in Ireland at the time) sent a Col. Venables to Belfast, which he took after a four-day siege. He then proceeded to turn the Presbyterian ministers not only out of the church but out of Belfast, and they would have to wait until the restoration of the monarchy in 1660 before being allowed back into Belfast.

When Col. Venables was in Belfast from 1649 to 1656, he took over the church and turned it into a citadel. He stabled his horses in it and took lead from the roof to make musket bullets. The church, although restored, would eventually be demolished in 1774 when St Anne's Church was being built in Donegall Street. The pulpit from the former Corporation Church was presented to St Mary's Catholic Church when it opened in 1784 and is still in full use there today.

The chair that King William III used when attending a service in the Corporation Church during his five-day stay in Belfast in June 1690 still survives and can be found to the left of the altar.

The pillars at the front of the church came from the Earl Bishop of Derry's unfinished house in Ballyscullon, County Londonderry. To the right of the chancel is a memorial to Sir Henry Pottinger who, in 1842, at the end of the Opium Wars in China, secured the lease of Hong Kong for the British government – a lease that only ran out in 1997.

When the Corporation Church was demolished in the 1770s, the graveyard remained and was the original burial place for Henry Joy McCracken, the United Irishman. In the early 1900s, Francis Joseph Biggar, solicitor and historian, re-interred McCracken's remains alongside his sister Mary Ann in Clifton Street Graveyard, upper section, Antrim Road Wall.

It is interesting to note that the new church, St Anne's, built in Donegall Street and paid for by the Earl of Donegall, was not complete when the Corporation Church was demolished in the 1770s. The First Presbyterian Church in Rosemary Street offered their building to the Church of Ireland for services. This was typical of this liberal church and was also a way of making amends, as the Presbyterians had taken over the former Corporation Church in 1644. This fine church is open most days until 2 p.m. and visitors are always welcome.

JOURNEY DOWN HIGH STREET FROM LOMBARD STREET TO VICTORIA STREET

No. 2: the present building replaced an 1868 building which housed an insurance company, and before that it was occupied by the chemists J. & W. Marshall, who acted as agents for the recently discovered Milk of Magnesia. There are still some old photographs that show some of the nineteenth-century shops on this site, including the famous Sawyers, in business from 1879. They eventually moved to Fountain Street and are now to be found in College Street.

Winecellar Entry is here, dating back to the seventeenth century and home to Whites Tavern.

Washington House (*c.* 1888): some of the buildings on this site were destroyed in the 1941 Belfast Blitz. The block from Washington House to the corner of Bridge Street houses three businesses. It is of no particular interest except as the location of one of the many entries that have been lost over the years: Orr's Entry between numbers 20 and 22 was lost in the 1941 Blitz.

Nos 42–46 (on the corner of High Street and Bridge Street): at one time a cinema was here, which opened in 1912. It closed due to bomb damage in the 1941 Blitz. In 1840 John Magee had premises at No. 46 that sold 'best London hats'. Magee was also the originator of a heavy overcoat in the 1860s called the 'Ulster'.

The historic Sugarhouse Entry is here, the meeting place of the United Irishmen.

River House: built on the site of buildings destroyed in the 1941 Blitz. One of the shops was that of a Joseph Lee, a jeweller who would check the dates of chronometers using 'astronomical charts'.

No. 62, the National Bank Building: built in the 1890s, this beautiful building somehow avoided being destroyed in the Blitz of 1941. It is now part of the nearby Merchant Hotel empire and is a welcome addition to the social and life of central Belfast.

Skipper Street: eighteenth-century ship's captains lodged here.

Nos 76–90 were demolished in 2008 and the site was developed as part of the Merchant Hotel.

Nos 96–98, Ulster Sports Club (1935): a favourite haunt of the late George Best and his dad when George paid one of his many visits home to his native city. The club was established in 1927 and moved here in 1935.

No. 100: destroyed in the Blitz.

Just off High Street is a little laneway previously called George Mitchell Entry. It was named after a nineteenth-century banker, not the famous Senator George Mitchell, the architect of the Good Friday Agreement.

No. 102, Transport House (at the corner with Victoria Street): the 1959 masterpiece by J.J. Brennan and built as the former HQ of the

Transport and General Workers Union/Unite, it contains the famous murals running the full height of the five-storey building depicting giant, marching workers, cranes, etc.

CASTLE PLACE

The history of Castle Place can be traced back to the Belfast of the 1600s, and it was once part of High Street. Many people do not realise that the original Belfast Castle, dating back to the twelfth century, was on the site were British Home Stores stands today. Hence the numerous references in the street names nearby: Castle Street, Castle Lane and Castle Arcade.

Castle Place: this street also known as Grand Parade in the 1790s as it was the venue for many military parades. It was also the area were public hangings took place. The last of these public hangings took place in the early nineteenth century and involved two men convicted of arson on premises in Peters Hill. Thomas Griffin records the event at the time: 'I remember distinctly seeing the helmets and swords of the Dragoons as their horses closed up the thoroughfare between High Street and Castle Place while the two men were hanged.'

On a lighter note, when trams were introduced, initially horse drawn and then in 1904 electric, Castle Place became more well known as Castle Junction. Even today many of the older citizens of Belfast still refer to it by that name. (The last tram to run in Belfast was in 1954. They were replaced by trolley and petrol-driven buses.)

A structure that stands out as a striking piece of architecture is the Bank Building (1899) This is the third version of this building and is today the home of Primark. The first version was built in 1787, and the second version in 1855. The original names of the owners of the 1899 building can still be seen above the present-day entrance: Robertson, Ledlie, and Ferguson.

The first Bank Building of 1787 was the brainchild of four bankers, all with the Christian name John and all members of the First Presbyterian Church in Rosemary Street. They started off in Castle Place approximately where HMV is today, then moved to Ann Street and were known as the 'Bank of the Four Johns'. They would move from Ann Street to the Bank Buildings and remain in business until it was dissolved in 1797. For a period the building was the home of a Church of Ireland bishop.

CASTLE PLACE AND HEADING DOWN TO CORNMARKET

Currys: the site now occupied by Currys and HMV (1990) was originally the famous Robbs Department Store. Even more interesting is the fact that the Donegall Arms Hotel, built in 1786, was absorbed into the Robb's building in the nineteenth century. The hotel was used by the army during the 1798 uprising and the last owner of the hotel was a man called Moore who is buried in Clifton Street Graveyard (his burial headstone is beside the Ewarts' plot on the dividing wall in the lower section).

BRIDGE STREET

This is one of the oldest streets in Belfast. It is shown on a map of 1680 and its name is derived from the stone bridge that crossed over the river Farset, also known as the Belfast river, at the High Street end. Bridge Street was also known as Cross Street and Broad Street.

In 1737 at the Sign of the Peacock, Francis Joy founded the *Belfast News Letter*, still published today.

In 1696 James Blow was invited over from Scotland, shortly after the arrival of King William III in Belfast. Blow had a print shop in the street. He is reputed to have published the first Bible in Ireland in 1704 but this is disputed as there is evidence that it was not published until much later.

HIGH STREET

Nos 1–21: built in 1957–59 on what was a blitzed site.

No. 1: above this building is a blue plaque commemorating that Sir James Murray, the inventor of Milk of Magnesia, had his apothecary shop nearby in High Street. He had been experimenting with liquid magnesium and offered this concoction to the visiting Lord Lieutenant, the Earl of Anglesey, to relieve his indigestion. While Sir James Murray's two sons are buried in Clifton Street Graveyard he was buried in Dublin.

Moving on down the block we find the excellent Barnardos Café, 'Dr B's', which offers training in the catering trade to young people with learning difficulties.

THE OTHER SIDE OF BRIDGE STREET STARTING AT THE NORTHERN WHIG PUB AND RESTAURANT

The building was completed in 1820 and was known as 'Commercial Buildings' as it was used by merchants as offices. In part of the building that fronts onto Waring Street there was a hotel (it is now the home of Clanmill Housing). The ground floor is a restaurant and pub called the Northern Whig (the founder of the *Northern Whig* newspaper, Francis Dalzell Finlay, is buried in Clifton Street Graveyard). It is a very popular venue with the local population and the ever-increasing number of tourists now visiting Belfast. Inside the building you will see three very imposing east European revolutionary figures.

Nos 12–16: built in 1955 on a bomb site for the famous Arnott's Store, which had been in business on the site since the 1860s. This present building was the home of Arnott's until 1974; they still have a store in Dublin.

Bridge Street was originally a much narrower street and was only widened in the reconstruction that took place after the Second World War.

ROSEMARY STREET (NAMED AFTER THE HERB)

This links Royal Avenue to Bridge Street. It is shown partially developed on a 1685 map, up to the back gardens of houses in what was then Hercules Lean (today Royal Avenue).

Rosemary Street is full of the history of Belfast and at one time boasted three Presbyterian churches. The First Presbyterian Church on the site dates back to 1695. The present building, the third, dates back to 1783 and was the brainchild of the minister at the time, Dr Crombie, along with the architect Roger Mulholland. The beautiful elliptical shape of the church is a joy to see (it is open on Wednesdays from 10 a.m. to 1 p.m. for short tours). Dr Crombie also founded the academy in 1785 and was its first principal. The school moved in the nineteenth century from Academy Street to its present home on the Cliftonville Road and is now known as the Belfast Royal Academy.

The historical First Presbyterian Church reflected the industrial, political and social life of Belfast in the eighteenth, nineteenth and twentieth centuries. Amongst its many members were:

- Sir Edward Harland
- Thomas Andrews Jnr, chief designer of the *Titanic*
- Dr William Drennan, founder of the United Irishmen*
- Francis Dalzell Finlay, owner of the *Northern Whig* newspaper*
- Thomas McCabe (United Irishman), a goldsmith and watchmaker at 6 North Street, Belfast, who in 1786 prevented a slave-ship company being set up in Belfast. Wolfe Tone referred to McCabe as 'the Irish Slave'*
- Mr Heron, one of the founders of the Ulster Bank*
- Members of the Joy Family, associated with the *Belfast News Letter*
- Montgomery, one of the founders of the Northern Bank*
- Marcus Ward Family, printers*

(* = Buried in Clifton Street Graveyard)

John Wesley preached here on Monday 8 June 1789. This church has always had a long tradition of free-thinking liberal attitudes.

The First and Second Presbyterian Churches (the second church, opened in 1708, was at the rear of the first) were non-subscribing Presbyterian churches, meaning they did not subscribe to the Westminster Confession of Faith although they agreed with parts of it. Some members of the first and second churches left to form the third because they did subscribe. When the third church was lost in the Blitz of 1941 its members moved to the North Circular Road in North Belfast but still kept the old connection, as the church is called Rosemary Church. The famous Irish patriot Henry Joy McCracken was a member of the Third Presbyterian Church. The Second Presbyterian Church closed in 1896 and can now be found in Elmwood Avenue and is known as All Souls. Its members, like those of the Third Church, kept the connection to their original home in Rosemary Street as their church hall is called Rosemary Hall. On 19 October 2008 the church celebrated its tercentenary.

The First Presbyterian Church is the only survivor of the three churches that used to grace this street. It is still today a full working church.

Nos 1–7, corner of Rosemary Street and North Street: Co-Op Travel Agency. This was the site of a sugarhouse in the eighteenth century. Later it was the site of the Stag's Inn, owned by Dan Miskelly from 1819 to 1839. He would advertise, in the local press, cheap travel to and from Coleraine. He is buried in Friar's Bush Graveyard.

No. 15, the Masonic Hall (1954): this was built on the site of the Third Presbyterian Church. A plaque, commemorating the famous

United Irishman, Henry Joy McCracken, is attached to the outside wall of the church. The McCracken family lived just across the road at the entrance to Winecellar Entry.

Nos 32–39, Central Hall (1958–59): part of the First Presbyterian Church replaced the manse that had been destroyed in the 1941 Blitz.

No. 41, First Presbyterian Church (1783): see above for description of this historic church.

A laneway leads to the Red Barn Gallery (Arts and Craft Shop): previously the Red Barn Pub (Gordon Sumner, better known as Sting, used to work as a barman here). The Red Barn Gallery offers an outlet for a variety of photographers and artists with free exhibitions to highlight their work. It also includes an archive of the history of photography in Belfast and many other places of interest throughout Ireland, some dating back to the early days of photography.

Nos 45–47: an attractive Italian-style building on the site of the former Second Presbyterian Church manse that now houses Donaghy & Carey Solicitors.

No. 49, Suitor Boutique: this boutique has seen many famous people from the film world pass through its doors, for example Brad Pitt, Barbara Streisland and Robin Williams, to name but a few. Some older folk may remember the pub called the Star and Garter that was previously on this site. There is a story that the pub previous to the Star and Garter had an underground passage to a cell under the Provost Marshall's house in High Street.

Just opposite the First Presbyterian Church, there was once an eighteenth-century theatre called the Playhouse Gate, just one of the many theatres to be found in Belfast in the eighteenth and nineteenth centuries.

WARING STREET

Waring Street is one of the streets shown on the Belfast map of 1685. It had many names, for example Broad Street and Wern Street. It is named after a tanner called William Waring from Toombridge, who was given a lease in 1670. He lived and carried on business in the street that bore his name. His daughter Jayne took the fancy of Jonathan Swift, a minister at the time in Kilroot. He refers to Jayne as 'Varina', but after two years Swift's advances were spurned and he headed back to England and eventually to Dublin. No. 2, Old Northern Bank (closed 2002): this was built as the Exchange in 1769 by the Earl of Donegal to celebrate the birth of his son George Augustus. The upper floors, i.e the Assembly Rooms, were added in 1776 by the famous London architect Robert Taylor. It was converted into a bank in 1845 by Charles Lanyon (architect of Queen's University). This building reflects a lot of the history of Belfast, for example:

Nos 10–12: The block from the corner of Waring and Donegall Street up to Hill Street is dominated by just two buildings. The site is part of a new Premier Inn hotel. On the ground floor is the new 4 Corners Restaurant. Back in the early 1800s it was the site of the Belfast Bank, before they moved across the road in 1845 to the former Exchange and Assembly Building. The new owners have lovingly restored the exterior of this nineteenth-century building and incorporated it into the new hotel.

HILL STREET

Cotton Court: a restored building that is set back from the street. It acknowledges the cotton trade that thrived in Belfast in the late eighteenth century. The cotton trade had originally been introduced into the poor house by Thomas McCabe, Captain John McCracken and Robert Joy as a means of employment and training for the residents.

The cotton industry in Belfast reached its peak in the 1820s but, due to fierce competition from the many mills in Lancashire, it was eclipsed by linen production from 1830 on.

On the kerbside is a very useful information board highlighting some of the history of the street, with a reference to Jonathan Swift.

The lower end of Waring Street terminates at Donegall Quay, where a stunning twenty-four-storey building now stands.

WARING STREET FROM THE CORNER OF BRIDGE STREET

Nos 1–3: built in 1819–20 and paid for by public subscriptions, costing £20,000, it was named Commercial Building and was used by Belfast merchants. It also contained a hotel at the corner of Waring Street and Sugarhouse Entry (were Clanmill Housing now have their offices). The Commercial Building was built on the site of four thatched cottages, one of which belonged to Samuel Neilson, who, like many Belfast Presbyterians, was a United Irishman. He carried on a successful woollen drapery business before being arrested for his membership of the United Irishmen in 1796.

The Commercial Building became the home of the *Northern Whig* when Francis Dalzell Finlay moved his newspaper there in the early nineteenth century. The *Northern Whig* ceased publishing as a newspaper in 1963.

Today the ground floor of the building is a bar and restaurant, still retaining the old name of the Northern Whig. In one of the many offices on the upper floors is the home of Martin Lynch and his production company Green Shoot Productions, aided and abetted by Deirdre Ashe. Martin Lynch is a well-known playwright with many plays under his belt.

Continuing down the street, we pass Sugarhouse Entry, famous in the eighteenth century for Peggy Barclay's Benjamin Franklin Tavern. The United Irishmen, all Presbyterians, met here using the cover name of 'The Muddlers Club'.

Nos 23–31, Cathedral House: on the gable wall of this building is a striking, full-length mural well worth having a look at.

No. 33, the Ulster Building (1869): at the corner of Skipper Street and Waring Street built in 1869, this small, three-storey building was once part of the former Ulster Bank headquarters next door but it is now, along with its neighbour, part of a hotel called The Merchant and is known as the Cloth Ear Public House. The new owners spent around £9 million renovating it into a luxury hotel and the magnificent chandelier at the entrance is a sight to behold.

Nos 35–39, the main building and the former Ulster Bank headquarters built in the late 1850s when this area was the commercial heart of the town: the exterior of the building has not been altered during its transformation into the magnificent Merchant Hotel. 'Britannia with Justice and Commerce' can still be seen on top of the building. Take a look at the railings at the entrance to the hotel, which feature the famous 'Red Hand of Ulster' – it is showing the left hand when it should be the right. This mistake was again repeated above the main entrance to the hotel, but as the architect was from Glasgow he might not have been aware of the significance of his mistake. The Merchant Hotel is a welcome addition to Belfast's growing capacity for accommodation and the new owners have to be congratulated for a magnificent restoration of this historic building. Parked at the front of the building is the hotel's Bentley, which can be hired to collect you from the airport. (If you get the chance to visit that 'jewel in the crown' of historic graveyards, i.e Clifton Street Graveyard, there you will find the grave of Mr Heron, one of the founders of the Ulster Bank.)

Waring Street continues on across Victoria Street, down as far as Donegall Quay.

DONEGALL STREET TO NORTH QUEEN STREET

This probably dates back to the 1750s and runs all the way up to Carrick Hill and North Queen Street from Waring Street. Its original name was Linenhall Street, as it contained a linen mill on the site of the present-day St Anne's Cathedral. By 1819 it was known as Donegall Street.

No. 1: the new Premier Inn hotel opened by the First Minister, Peter Robinson, in October 2008. The façade of the original nineteenth-century building has been incorporated into the new hotel. At one time in the early 1800s it was the home of the Belfast Bank, which later became the Belfast Banking Company, moving across the road in 1845 to the old Exchange and Assembly Building.

Next door is the former Eason's Building, dating back to the 1950s. Eason's had been on this site back to about 1895. Just opposite, in 1972, is the site of the first car-bomb explosion in Belfast – six dead and over 100 injured.

No. 25 (*c.* 1760): this is a historic building restored by the former Laganside Development Corporation. Back in the 1790s, Martha McTier was part of a ladies committee who were setting up a lying-in hospital (maternity hospital) in this building for 'respectable' working-class women to give birth. The lying-in hospital later moved to a purpose-built hospital on ground donated by the Belfast Charitable Society in Clifton Street in 1830, then to Townsend Street and finally to its present home on the Royal Victoria Hospital site. (Note that the RVH is the second largest hospital in the UK, covering over 70 acres – the largest is St Jimmy's in Leeds.)

Exchange Place is here (an existing eighteenth-century entry leading to Hill Street).

No. 27 (late eighteenth century): in 1890 the *Morning News* and *Weekly Examiner* were published here.

Nos 45–47, Resource Centre (including Foster College): advice centre for the unemployed (owners of the John Hewitt pub – a popular meeting place for writers, musicians, etc.).

Donegall Street Place is here: look down the passageway to see the James Larkin sculpture by Anto Brennan and on the wall behind a magnificent mural.

Nos 49–67: the former premises of the *Belfast News Letter* (*c.* 1872), founded at the Sign of the Peacock in Bridge Street by Francis Joy in September 1737 and which is reputed to be the oldest English-language newspaper still in production.

Talbot Street is here.

St Anne's Cathedral (1898–2007): the magnificent St Anne's Cathedral is built on the site of two former buildings. One was a brown linen hall which was replaced by St Anne's Church. The church was opened in 1776 and was designed by the architect Francis Horne, assisted by Andrew Mulholland and paid for by Lord Donegall, an absentee landlord who took a great interest in Belfast's development. The cathedral was started in 1898 with the tower being removed from the old church, where services continued until 1903. The first architect to work on St Anne's was Sir Thomas Drew, one of eight architects to work on this magnificent building. After the installation of the modern-style steeple in 2007 the Cathedral can now be said to be complete. (When you look at the complete destruction of the nearby buildings in the 1941 Blitz, it is something of a miracle that St Anne's is still here today.)

Academy Street here leads up to York Street.

No. 77: this was the original site of the academy founded in 1785 by Revd Dr Crombie, minister of the First Presbyterian Church in Rosemary Street. The academy moved to its present site on the Cliftonville Road in 1878 and is known today as Belfast Royal Academy. The present-day site of the school includes the Crombie Building in remembrance of its founder.

Nos 79–93, present-day public park featuring the 'Three Buoys': it backs onto the excellent refurbished University of Ulster Art College. The well-known architectural practice Barry Todd Architects of Hill Street carried out this work. Within a few years, 12,500 students are due to move from the University of Ulster, Jordanstown, campus into the extended York Street Campus.

This section of Donegall Street housed various buildings including the International Bar at the corner with York Street, which was destroyed in the Belfast Blitz.

Donegall Street Congregational Church has recently changed hands but is still one of the many churches in Belfast city centre that holds services on Sundays. This site goes back to the early 1800s, where in 1831 the Institute for the Deaf and Dumb and Blind was founded. The institute moved to a site on the Lisburn Road in the 1840s (replaced by the present-day Queen's Medical Biology Centre). The Donegall Street church has been rebuilt and altered many times and at one time extended much further out into the street.

Nos 113–17, 'The Irish News' (*c.* 1905): built on the site of a nineteenth-century building belonging to John McCracken (member of the famous McCracken family). Next door is the famous Clark School of Dancing.

Donegall Lane is here.

Nos 193–95, two former schools (1828): Christian Brothers (boys) and National School (boys and girls), built in the Gothic style. These buildings were almost lost in a fire. The flames also spread to St Patrick's Church next door, which was fortunately saved from complete destruction by the Fire Service. Both buildings are still in use today.

St Patrick's Church: this present, magnificent building in Gothic style dates back to 1874–77. The original church, consecrated in 1815, was the second Catholic church to be re-established in the town of Belfast. Another fascinating fact is that members of the Protestant community in Belfast contributed to the building costs.

The present St Patrick's Church contains a famous painting, *The Madonna of the Lakes* by Sir John Lavery, who was born just off North Queen Street. Because of this connection to the area, his wife Helen suggested donating the painting to the church. Helen Lavery, her daughter and step-daughter sat for the painting. Helen was the Madonna and the two daughters are St Patrick and St Brigid. This famous painting can be found at the left-hand side of the church. Incidentally, John Lavery got the idea for the painting from the *Madonna of the Lakes* statue in Killarney. Helen Lavery is the lady who appeared on the Irish pound notes as Cathleen Na Houlihan. Also in the church to the left of the altar is the walled tomb of Bishop Dorrian, Bishop of Down and Connor in the nineteenth century. If you look to the right-hand side of the church you will see, in the stained-glass window, a representation of the first church on this site, i.e the 1815 church.

Above the entrance to the church is a statue of St Patrick which was sculpted by Patrick Pearse's father, an Englishman, who was an ecclesiastical sculptor working in Ireland at the time.

No. 199, St Patrick's Presbytery: built in 1820 with a magnificent brass door showing the scars of a huge bomb that destroyed a building across the road during the recent troubles, it was originally the Bishop of Down and Connor's Palace.

Nos 201–5, the remainder of a block of beautiful Georgian houses dating back to 1820 (the site dates back to the 1790s): we have to thank the Hearth Housing Association for the restoration of thee houses, which have been rented out. Number 201 is used by St Patrick's Church.

Nos 207–15 were lost to a road-widening scheme in 1990. No. 215 was where Belfast High School had its beginnings, originally known as Mercantile College. It moved to Glenravel Street, eventually became known as Belfast High School and can now be found in Greenisland, just past the entrance to the University of Ulster campus at Jordanstown. This finishes the journey up Donegall Street to North Queen Street.

LOWER DONEGALL STREET TO CARRICK HILL

The old Exchange and Assembly Buildings at the corner with Waring Street date back to 1769–76.

Nos 20–22: this building dates back to 1920 but was the site of the Brown Linen Hall, which was originally located where St Anne's Cathedral is today. It was moved to allow the 1775 St Anne's Church to be built, paid for by the Earl of Donegall.

North Street Arcade: opened in 1936, this well-known arcade that housed many small businesses was destroyed by arsonists in 2004 and now lies derelict. The mid-nineteenth-century Brookfield Linen Company Building was on this site. Even today if you look above the entrance there is an original plaque referring to its former use.

No. 36: the site dates back to the 1760s when it was the home of the famous liberal educationalist David Manson. It was later used by the Provincial Bank of Ireland. Today it is the site of a modern building.

The large open area facing St Anne's Cathedral is now known as 'Writers Square' and is the venue for many festival activities.

Nos 60–68, Cathedral Buildings: the Fourth Presbyterian Church could found on this site in 1791.

No. 96: the famous McGlades Bar was originally on this site, which then became the Penny Farthing. Both were popular with the journalists of the many newspapers nearby. The original name of the pub when it first opened was The Arcade Bar, as it ran from Donegall Street to Library Street. Today, after refurbishment, it is known as the Kremlin, with an imposing statue of Lenin above the entrance.

Union Street is here.

Nos 106–8: McEllhatton's Bar, known as the 'Front Page', dates back to 1910 and is a popular venue for music. It was also popular with journalists.

No. 112: Turkish baths stood on this site in around 1860.

Nos 114–18: the famous Hugh O'Kane & Co., dating back to 1865, still use, on certain occasions, beautiful black horses to pull the hearses. These were a common sight up to the 1950s.

Nos 120–38, Marsh Building (1894) with shops on the ground floor: One of the most interesting shops was Marshall's (directly next door to O'Kane's). It was famous for the supply of many foreign newspapers and magazines. If you look above the modern facade of the present-day shop you can see that the original name has survived.

The building next door was destroyed by a bomb in the 1970s, causing a large piece of wood to become embedded in the structure of

St Patrick's Church across the road. The site is now a private car park.

The previous corner building is now part of a car park that borders Donegall Street and Carrick Hill.

Our journey along Donegall Street from Waring Street to Carrick Hill is now complete.

SOME SHORTER DESCRIPTIONS OF SOME OF THE MANY OTHER LANES AND STREETS OF BELFAST

Sandy Row

It is an appropriate name for an area that stood on the banks of the Blackstaff river. When Sir Arthur Chichester, in 1612, built his castle in the centre of the town, 1,200,000 bricks used in the building came from Sandy Row. The street runs from Durham Street to the Lisburn Road.

Soap Lean/Lane

This is shown on a 1715 map, and the name refers to the old soap works that was located at the junction of Hill Street and Talbot Street but is now only a memory, as it was demolished.

Adelaide Street (also known as Stephen's Street)

Adelaide Street is named after one of the daughters of Queen Victoria. It runs from the back of the City Hall up to Ormeau Avenue. The previous name, Stephen's Street, refers to Stephen McLean, related to the ruling Donegall family through marriage.

Nos 10–20: this was the former home to the famous whiskey producers Dunville & Co. The company had to approach the priest in nearby St Malachy's Church to reduce the tolling of the church bells as it was affecting the whiskey in their bonded warehouse. Unfortunately the minor disturbance of tolling church bells became irrelevant when Belfast was blitzed by German bombs in April and May 1941 and the building was completely destroyed.

Nos 27–37: the company of Ireland Brothers specialised in 'splendiferous white linen for the uniforms of South American admirals and field marshalls'.

Ashburne Mews/Ashburne Street/Ashburne Place

This was named in honour of Edward Gibson, Baron Ashbourne, Lord Chancellor of Ireland 1885–1905. It runs from Salisbury Street to Maryville Street, and was redeveloped in 1985.

Coles Alley
This is shown on a 1757 map with other names, i.e Little Lane and Coal Lane. It has been known as Coles Alley from 1861. The entry runs from Church Lane to Ann Street and at one time contained twelve small houses. It was the home of Mrs Mellon, an actress who appeared in performances in the Vault Theatre in nearby Ann Street. Her daughter Harriet was also an actress but married the head of Coutts Bank (the Royal Family's Bank). Harriet would later, after her husband's death, become the Duchess of St Alban's. All twelve houses were destroyed in the 1941 Blitz.

Squeeze Gut Entry
This is an eighteenth-century street just off Castle Street in the heart of the city, so called because it was a narrow entry where people would have to squeeze to get past each other. The name was changed, for obvious reasons, and it is now known as College Court.

Cow Lane
Today known as Victoria Street, its history goes back to the time when cows were driven down to the Strand (the shoreline of the river Lagan) to graze.

Bank Street
Also known as Bank Lane and 'Back of the River'; there are two stories for this name: (1) there was a bank at the corner with Castle Place, and (2) it was once known as 'Back of the River', because the river Farset/Belfast river flowed down the street on its way to the river Lagan.

Royal Avenue
This was originally a long, narrow street called Hercules Street, named after Sir Hercules Langford, a Mayor of Belfast. It was opened up in the 1870s into a broad avenue. Up to 4,000 people had to be moved to allow for this development.

Donegall Pass
Also known as Pass Loning: Belfast in the early 1600s was still partially covered by woods, and so the Earl of Donegall opened up six pathways or 'lonings' through the woods to allow access from one road to another.

Falls Road
The name is derived from the Irish words *Tuath-na-bhfal* – a district

of falls or hedges.

Callendar Street
The name has nothing to do with days and months but refers to a process by which calico was 'calendered'. The street runs from Castle Lane to Chichester Street.

Academy Street
(From Donegall Street to Hill Street) in 1785 Revd Dr Crombie, minister of the First Presbyterian Church in Rosemary Street, opened an Academy alongside St Anne's Church. As minister of the church he was also headmaster of the school. When he died, Revd Bruce took over both as minister and as headmaster of the school. The academy moved in the nineteenth century to the Cliftonville Road in the north of the city. It is now known as the Belfast Royal Academy.

Chapel Lane (also known as Crooked Lane)
This runs from Berry Street to Castle Street. The name reflects that in 1784 a Catholic church, St Mary's, was opened on a site leased by the Earl of Donegall. Its original name was Crooked Lane as it has a slight bend.

Garfield Street
This street runs from North Street to Royal Avenue. It is not well known that it is named after an American president who was assassinated in the nineteenth century. The members of the nearby Presbyterian Church in Rosemary Street approached the family for permission to commemorate his name in the street.

Mill Street
This street was an extension of Castle Street and was so called because in the later 1500s an Elizabethan mill was erected to take advantage of the river Farset, which passed by on its way through Belfast to the river Lagan.

Frederick Street
Running from York Street to Nelson Street, this is one of the many streets with names relating to the Royal Family. It was the site of the last thatched cottage to survive from the early development of Belfast in the early 1600s, and, although it may be an urban myth, it is claimed that a prominent United Irishman took refuge in the cottage during the turbulent days of the late eighteenth century.

The Four Corners

This appropriately highlights the meeting of four of the seventeenth century streets: Bridge Street, Rosemary Street, North Street and Waring Street in the heart of Belfast. There is some confusion about whether the nearby Donegall Street is included, but that is a much later, eighteenth-century street.

North Street

This was also called Goose Lane, dating back to the time when a wall was built around Belfast in 1642. The geese would be let out through the North Gate into the nearby fields.

Berry Street

Also known as Factory Row, this street runs from Royal Avenue to Smithfield Square. The proper name for the street is Berry Street as it was named for an agent who represented the Donegall Family after they moved to England in the 1720s. It is also famous as the location of the first fever hospital to be opened in Ireland in 1792 and as the site of Berry Street Meeting House. This meeting house was replaced in the mid-nineteenth century by the present-day building.

Ballymacarret

In the east of the city, approached by the many bridges across the Lagan, is an area called Ballymacarret. Its name is derived from the Irish for the town of McArt (Bally or Bailie means townland).

Linenhall Street

There were three different locations for this name. The first was a street that ran from Waring Street to York Street and was opened up by the Earl of Donegall in the late eighteenth century. The second location was the street that led up to the White Linen Hall, which opened in 1785. This street passed through what had been part of the old castle gardens. When this street was renamed Donegall Place, the Linenhall name transferred permanently to the back of the present-day City Hall, where it runs up to Ormeau Road (*Ormeau* is French for 'young elms').

Corn Market

This was also called the 'Shambles', a reference to butchers trading in the area. The night mail coach to Dublin would leave from the Plough Hotel in Cornmarket.

Malone Road

This begins its journey from Bradbury Place, heading to the outskirts of the town.

Dargan's Island

This island was created when the channel out of Belfast to the sea was dredged and the sludge was developed into an island on the east side of the city. This land, now part of Harland and Wolff Shipbuilding, was once home to Belfast's answer to London's Crystal Palace. It was renamed Queen's Island to commemorate Queen Victoria's 1848 visit. It included a public park and a zoological collection with the shallow water nearby used for bathing. People attending the park would be ferried across the river for one old halfpenny.

Townsend Street

'Townsend' simply denoted where the town ended. It lies just off Peters Hill and leads to Divis Street.

Lilliput Street

This name ties in with the time when Jonathan Swift, who was a minister in Kilroot just outside Carrickfergus, would travel along the Belfast shoreline to visit his girlfriend Jayne Waring, 'Varina', in the town. An old map records a farm in this area called Lilliput Farm. It is also where he would have observed the outline of the Cavehill and its resemblance to a giant lying asleep, which he used in his book *Gulliver's Travels*.

Shankill Road

This is a name that reflects the old history of Belfast. Before the Reformation of the sixteenth century, the mother church of the Catholic Church in Belfast was situated approximately where the present-day Shankill Graveyard and the nearby St Matthew's Church now lie. This road was also the main route out of Belfast to Antrim some 20 miles away. When in the 1830s a more direct route was established it was agreed that there should not be two roads with the same name. It was suggested and accepted that with the former connection to the sixteenth-century Catholic mother church of Belfast, it should be called 'Shankill', which is Irish for 'Old Church'.

THE SMITHFIELD AND LIBRARY DISTRICT OF BELFAST

This area can trace its history back to the seventeenth century.

Library Street

A narrow street off Royal Avenue developed in 1788. On a 1791 map it is shown as Mustard Street, named from Richard Calwell's mustard factory. From 1861 to 1890 there were over eighty small houses in the street occupied by E.G. Tobacco Spinners and a blacksmith. With the opening in 1880 of the nearby John Street (which became part of the extended Royal Avenue), many of the houses were demolished and the street was renamed Library Street, from the new public library nearby in Royal Avenue.

Kent Street

This was originally called Margaret Street, as shown on the 1791 map. It was renamed Kent Street around 1840 and at one time contained over forty small houses, many of which were occupied by weavers employed in the Kent Street Linen Factory. At numbers 23–27 was the Kent Street National School, founded in the 1870s. The last remaining houses – numbers 34–38, built in the 1830s, were demolished in 1992.

Gresham Street

On the 1791 map this is shown as Hudson's Entry, named after the tanner Christopher Hudson, who in 1788 leased land in nearby Smithfield Square. In 1820 it contained fifty-five houses, but by 1852 it was described by the writer O'Hanlon as 'a complete den of vice and uncleanness, probably only unsurpassed in what is called the civilised world'. In 1880 the street was enlarged and renamed Gresham Street. There were two pet shops that survived right up to the 1980s: Montgomery's, and next door, Creighton's. The owner Creighton had been a former unsuccessful boxer in his day and had the nickname 'Birdseed Creighton'. The nearby Hudson's Bar pays homage to the original name. The origin of the present name of the street can be traced back to a building in nearby Royal Avenue that was the home of the Gresham Life Office and was probably the reason for the name change.

Union Street

The street dates back to 1788 and was completely developed by 1891. It once housed a mixture of businesses, such as marine stores, coffin makers and undertakers, quill manufacturers and bellow makers. In 1894 Kennedy and Morrison's Warehouse stood at the corner of Kent Street and dealt in railway furnishings. They were also agents for boxwood and oil. Next door was a company called Frederick King, selling 'Edwards Desiccated Soap and Preserved Potato'. They also supplied piccalillis made with 'Spices from the Orient', which actually came from the Orient Farm near Comber!

Upper North Street

This is one of the original streets of old Belfast and is recorded on a 1665 map. Near the top of the street, close to Carrick Hill, stood the Gaiety Picture and Variety Theatre, which opened for business in 1916 but closed in 1956 to be replaced by a Woolworths store, which in turn is today a bingo hall.

Nos 132–40: Elephant Building, dating back to 1893. Many people will remember the elephant that once stood over the doorway of the off-licence, which is now just a memory. The whereabouts of the famous elephant is still a mystery.

Smithfield Square

This was laid out in 1788 and dominated by pubs and pawnbrokers. In 1848, Smithfield Market was a mixture of small shops in three covered arcades. Over the years it became a treasure house with many family businesses, for example Havlin's, Harry Hall, Hugh Greer, Conlon's Second Hand Furniture, Garvey's Bicycle Shop, Simmons the Jewellers and many, many more. In 1974 Smithfield Market was destroyed and the new Smithfield Market in Winetavern Street is still cutting its teeth, but will in any case find it hard to exert the same appeal or drawing power as the original.

Winetavern Street

A late eighteenth-century street, there is some evidence that its former name was Pipe Lane, reflecting the number of pipe workers that worked there. In 1813 it is listed as Winetavern Street and housed the Winetavern Street Mill, which was later known as the Smithfield Flax Spinning and Weaving Co. Ltd.

BIBLIOGRAPHY

BOOKS

Agnew, J. (1995) *Funeral Register of the First Presbyterian Church*, Ulster Historical Foundation.
Agnew, J. (1996) *Belfast Merchant Families in the 17th Century*, Four Courts Press.
Bardon, J. (1982) *Belfast: An Illustrated History*, Blackstaff Press.
Bardon, Dr Jonathan (2002) *An Interesting and Honourable History*, Belfast Charitable Society.
Bardon, Jonathan & Conlin, Stephen (1995) *Belfast, 1000 Years*, Blackstaff Press.
Beckett, J.C. (1988) *Belfast: The Making of a City*, Appletree Press.
Benn, George (1877) *History of Belfast*, Marcus Ward & Co.
Benn, G. (1887) *A History of the Town of Belfast.*
Bradbury, John (2002) *Celebrated Citizens of Belfast*, Appletree Press.
Chart, D.A. (1931) *The Drennan Letters*, HMSO.
Clarke, R.S.J. & Merrick, A.C.W. (1984) *Gravestone Inscriptions*, Ulster Historical Foundation.
Connolly, S.J. (1998) *The Oxford Companion to Irish History*, Oxford University Press.
Erskine, J. & Lucy, G. (1997) *Cultural Traditions in N. Ireland*, QUB Institute of Irish Studies.
Gillespie, Raymond & Royle, Stephen A. (2008) *Irish Historic Towns Atlas No. 12, Belfast, Part 1, to 1840*, Royal Irish Academy.
Gordon, Revd A. (1887) *Historic Memorials of the First. Presbyterian Church of Belfast*, Marcus Ward & Co.: Royal Ulster Works.
Gray, J. & McCann, W. (1996) *An Uncommon Man*, Linen Hall Library.

Holmes, R. Finlay (1981) *Henry Cooke*, Christian Journals Ltd.
Killen, J. (1998) *The United Irishmen and the Government of Ireland 1791–1801*, Linen Hall Library.
Larkin, J. (ed.) (1991) *The Trial of William Drennan*, Irish Academic Press.
Larmour, Paul (1987) *Belfast: An Illustrated Architectural Guide*, Friar's Bush Press.
McCavitt, Dr P. (1998) *Sir Arthur Chichester*, Institute of Irish Studies.
McKay, Dr P. (1999) *A Dictionary of Place Names*, QUB Institute of Irish Studies.
McNally, Kenneth (1972) *The Narrow Streets*, Blackstaff Press.
McNeill, T. (1980) *Anglo Norman Ulster: The History and Archaeology of an Irish Barony 1177–1400*, QUB Institute of Irish Studies.
Magee, John (1992) *The Heritage of the Harp*, Linenhall Library.
Maguire, W.A. & Speers, S. (1998) *Belfast: Site and City*, Ulster Museum.
Merrick, A.C.W., edited by Clarke, R.S.J. (1991) *Old Belfast Families and the New Burying Ground*, Ulster Historical Foundation.
Millin, Shannon (1931) *Side Lights on the History of Belfast*, W. & G. Baird.
Newman, K. (1993) *Dictionary of Ulster Biography*, QUB Institute of Irish Studies.
O'Byrne, C. (1946) *As I Roved Out*, Universities Press Ltd.
O'Regan, Raymond (2006) *First Presbyterian Church of Belfast from 1644: A Revision of Tom Moore's History*, Queen's University, in-house publication.
O'Regan, Raymond (2006) *Quote Unquote: A Selection of Letters between Dr William Drennan to His Sister and Family in Belfast*, Queen's University, in-house publication.
O'Regan, Raymond (2006) *Samuel Neilson: The Forgotten Patriot*, Queen's University, in-house publication.
O'Regan, Raymond (2008) *Happy Birthday Queen's: Celebrating 100 Years of a Leading University*, Queen's University, in-house publication.
O'Regan, Raymond (2010) *Hidden Belfast*, Mercier Press.
O'Reilly, Des (2010) *Rivers of Belfast: A History*, Colour Print Books.
Patton, Marcus (1993) *Central Belfast: An Historical Heritage Gazetteer*, Ulster Architectural Heritage Society.
Pheonix, Eamon (2000) *Two Acres of Irish History: A Study Through Time of Friars Bush and Belfast 1750–1918*, Ulster Historical Foundation.